PREVIOUS BOOKS

AN ARTIFICIAL WILDERNESS

THE ELECTRIC LIFE

AMERICAN ENERGIES

THE GUTENBERG ELEGIES

READINGS

MY SKY BLUE TRADES

READING LIFE: BOOKS FOR THE AGES

THE ART OF TIME IN MEMOIR

THE OTHER WALK

CHANGING THE SUBJECT

SPEAK, MEMORY (BOOKMARKED)

THE MIRÓ WORM

and

THE MYSTERIES OF WRITING

ARROWSMITH PRESS

The Miró Worm and the Mysteries of Writing
© 2024 Sven Birkerts
All Rights Reserved

ISBN: 979-8-9904050-0-4

Library of Congress Control Number: 2024910779

Boston — New York — San Francisco — Baghdad
San Juan — Kyiv — Istanbul — Santiago, Chile
Beijing — Paris — London — Cairo — Madrid
Milan — Melbourne — Jerusalem — Darfur

11 Chestnut St.
Medford, MA 02155

arrowsmithpress@gmail.com
www.arrowsmithpress.com

The Sixty-First Arrowsmith book
was typeset & designed by Ezra Fox
for Askold Melnyczuk & Alex Johnson
in Garamond fonts

Front Cover Art © 2024 Sven Birkerts

"The Ghost of Electricity: The Dylan Face" first appeared in *Conjunctions.*
All other essays were lead pieces for AGNI.

THE MIRÓ WORM

and

THE MYSTERIES OF WRITING

Sven Birkerts

Contents

To Lynn, Mara and Liam, my family,

for humoring me for all these years

The Uncanny Valley

This introduction was written in the Precambrian era, which is to say quite recently but not recently enough. There is no recently enough, which ought to be the mantra for our galloping technological age, which almost daily produces systemic innovations that de-stabilize whatever was the most recent short-lived status quo.

I'm not talking about changes of degree here, but an overall change of kind. And I'm not being glib—what's happening in the tech field has Gutenberg-scaled implications. Deep-learning algorithms are already so sophisticated and empowered that any one can generate competent college essays, business reports, prospectuses, and almost anything else that needs generating. Almost.

It's the 'almost' that touches on the literary and raises the encompassing question: how far can programmed AI impinge on individual creativity? Can it produce serious artistic work that passes the AI Turing Test— work that a reader believes is human-authored? And if it can, then what? This issue was taken up in *AGNI 98* by my co-editor William Pierce, but it's important enough to warrant further questioning.

The great data engines are steadily churning and the self-refining programs are closing in fast. Last year the news broke that the works of thousands of literary writers are being gathered into a database to be purposefully digested. Algorithmic filters are picking out the markers of stylistic performance and widening the already impressive predictive reach. The work is—and this is outright theft—being appropriated *pro bono* and without permission from the writers.

As the gap narrows between AI-generated text and that of humans, nuances of expression become increasingly important. The merest shadings of tone, signature twists of diction—qualities that might elude the coders' best efforts—make the difference. The word I think of is 'asymptote,' which is defined in mathematics as a line that gets closer and closer to a given curve but never actually reaches it.

~

The ever-narrowing interval between man and machine was dramatically illustrated in the 2016 face-off between Japanese Go master Lee Sedol and Demis Hassabis' AI program AlphaGo, which has been documented in Benjamín Labatut's recent novel, *The Maniac*, which is very much about that interval. The five-game match played in Seoul was filmed and can be viewed online. Not surprisingly, it features long stretches where we see nothing but Sedol's face, his utterly immobile concentration. Such narrative momentum as is there is generated by shots of his hand placing a stone on the Go board, and his proxy opponent doing the same. And then, of course, the press box scenes where we see and hear the gathered experts annotating every move, calculating odds. Once we start to grasp the implication of the unfolding face-off, the tension quickly escalates.

Part of the tension comes from watching Sedol's initially brash confidence erode as he begins to grasp the power of his opponent. The set of his mouth is ever tighter. Shockingly, he loses the first three games. Sedol, losing! He stares at the board in disbelief. We feel the mood change perceptibly among the crowd of media commentators and fans.

In fact, something happens in the course of play that is more dramatic than Sedol's concession to the algorithm. A single telling—game-changing—move by the AI program in an early face-off. We see AlphaGo's proxy reach out and place a stone in an entirely unexpected place. Neither Sedol nor the team of expert onlookers can begin to fathom this. The move violates every accepted tenet of play; it's a historical first in tournament play. The room grows very still, the silence ticks. Sedol cannot seem to find a way to counter. It's in that time of standoff that he realizes that AlphaGo's move—irrational, unanticipated—is strategic in a special way. It is *creative*. The program appears to be thinking outside the expected parameters.

While Sedol loses the overall competition, he wins the fourth game by coming up with a bold and unlikely move that somehow flummoxes AlphaGo's ability to counter. The crowd erupts, its relief expressed through a collective roar. But to the invested observer it feels like a Pyrrhic victory, a mere token. That Sedol salvages one victory out of five suggests that the power of the program is not absolute. Sedol's one win has a purely symbolic value. There's a fine line drawn. He's the highest ranking Go master, but what about the rest of us?

~

Go is a mind game with certain rules and constraints. The threats now facing the writer are troubling in very different ways. Viewed in a larger frame, we find concerns about authorship and authenticity, what might be called the 'presenting problems.' Underneath are even more profound questions about the fate of individual expression and the ongoing viability of the age-old circuit between writer and reader.

The questions touch on so many things. The seeping of computer-generated text into our various language systems—who could have dreamed it?—can also be seen as a harbinger of a mentality that is taking over more and more of our discourse. Words treated as merely functional begin to lead us to a gradual acceptance of what might be called a streamlined adequacy. Predictive language models are tampering from the inside with what is often called the distinguishing feature of our species.

~

The issue of human language versus AI-generated language is complicated right from the outset by the fact that machine language is modeled on the human. 'Language,' the Latin *lingua*, was originally organized sounds produced by the human tongue. Words first turned on the tongue were eventually subjected to the logic of syntax and then gradually fashioned into script that could be read with the eye, and only much later still sounded out silently in the reader's mind.

Predictive language models manipulate words as if they were tokens in a game. Yet these machines quite often achieve a persuasive validity. This is owed in part to the genius of the technology—which is mind-bogglingly sophisticated—but there is also another, less-obvious, reason. These 'tokens' are drawn from languages that have evolved over millennia. A word is also a history, has a life comprised of usages. Some of that life can be felt in any sensible expression. As Emerson wrote, "Every word was once a poem." Unfortunately, using words only for their immediate designating value is a kind of strip-mining of what used to be called the 'word hoard,' leaching away much of the original sap.

Artificial language programs have as their blueprint the basic propositional logic of language. Algorithms crunch the repertoire of combinatory possibilities, and from these generate the necessary patterns of syntax. A predictive sequencing of words can create "meaning" in large part because these consumed words and phrases are already freighted with meanings. Used intentionally by humans, they carry some of the aura of their history, whereas a sentence that has been generated by an AI program really has no value beyond its basic designatory function. That seems obvious enough. But then who will ever know? Which is to say, in effect: who cares? Expressive intention is so readily assumed, even when it's not there. Does it matter? Will people continue to think it does?

~

AI-generated text cannot be traced back to any human agency, aside from the original coding that created the algorithm. The words are drawn from dictionaries and from the vast archive of the public—and copyrighted—domain. No one owns words. Conforming to established patterns of syntax, they can achieve a use-appropriate sense. It really is hard to tell that a machine assembled each sentence, and we're already at a point where we might start to wonder. The doubting reader occupies a highly uncertain state.

This state has been called, mysteriously, the *uncanny valley*, defined by Wikipedia as a hypothesis predicting that "any entity appearing almost human will risk eliciting cold, eerie feelings in viewers." Lacking the basic certainty about the status of a work, the reader experiences an unanchored expression, a diminished version of the traditional circuit of exchange, a sense that everything might now live inside parentheses. The uncanny valley is where our primary age-old connection to the language starts to thin out.

~

There is also the easily overlooked but highly important matter of projection. Projection is when the reader imposes onto a text qualities that may not be part of the work—impositions that may have everything to do with the reader's wants and needs. Projection makes a literary work come alive; it draws on the will to believe.

When I was ten or eleven, I was besotted with the *Hardy Boys* series, reading book after book about two brothers, Frank and Joe, who pass their days solving crimes in their home town of Bayport. Completely immersed in that world and its cast of recurring characters,

I lived the scenarios. Everything I encountered in my own waking day was clue-ridden, part of some crime network operating in my area. I marveled that author Franklin W. Dixon could produce good books at such a prodigious rate. I had awakened in myself the will to believe.

I learned later, after I was done with the series, that Franklin W. Dixon was a factory of hacks following proven formulas. A sad truth to realize in hindsight, but it confirms for me how much the will to believe and the assumption of authorial intent condition our reading. How else could I, critic-to-be, have read right past the boilerplate sentences and canned repetitions, the stock clichés— read past everything? I'm still embarrassed.

~

Language and the intelligence it enables are what distinguishes us from the rest of creation. "In the beginning was the word," if you will. I never thought to question that primacy—it was the bedrock underlying all things. I still believe it. But now it feels that the species barrier is being breached. The prose of our best writers is being hijacked, put to uses yet unknown. To what end?

Mysterious as the workings of machine learning may be themselves, the end appears obvious enough. Having already brought their programs to a reliable level of competence—creating a college essay that passes muster even at Harvard—AI programmers are taking up the next challenge. They are looking to endow machine-generated prose with style—to make it still more "human." If a writer's style is her fingerprint, they are looking for ways to make it part of their own. Style is, where the writer is concerned, identity.

~

I look at two identical sentences, one written by a person, the other generated by a sophisticated AI program. There is no difference. Words are what they are, they mean what they mean. And if I can't tell which is which, is there any issue? It would seem academic, moot. But in truth there is a very big issue. The sentences may be the same, but the not-knowing now casts a shadow. As soon as I suspect that one of the sentences has been machine-generated, my reception is affected. The uncanny valley. We face the issue of intention—which for long millennia has underlain all written expression. Was this written with an expressive aim in mind by a person?

I see intention as a strictly human attribute, different from a plan to be executed, or a set of instructions for some result that can be followed— something an AI program can propose for itself and fulfill. However competent the digital-language program, something is missing where expressive writing is concerned. While a project can be proposed and completed by way of reason—algorithmic can-do— intent originates in human need or desire. If the objective aim is to describe a course of treatment or the rules of chess, that is easily met. But if it is to explain why a painting or musical composition or poem is successful—in other words, if it is evaluative—the program may seem to succeed, but the result is all appearance. Any response that is evaluative has to be rooted in the self-aware subjectivity of the holder.

An AI program can't achieve the discriminations that are at some level rooted in the physical body. Emily Dickinson cited poems that made the reader feel like their head would come off. She was talking about sound, rhythm, and associative nuance. The program might respond by noting a reference or two from mythology, but can it account for the nature of the connection, how it feeds the poem?

When the AlphaGo program seemed to verge on being a human intelligence, it was because of the one move, the anomaly, the placing of a stone outside the reach of predictive calculation. And when Sedol made his one winning gambit, it was also out of the range of human predictability—far enough out to confound AlphaGo's algorithms.

This suggests, from one side and the other, that the anomaly can be a crucial indicator. Writer Bill Pierce recently took up the question from a different perspective:

I just finished Annie Ernaux's account of her abortion in the early 1960s,
Happening, *and it will easily help me express what I've been groping for.
AI will never write a book that tells us something. . . new about being
human—something recognizably true yet so personal as to be unheard
of. That combination is a hallmark: familiarity—I can feel the open-
palmed, non-plussed, frustrated truth-telling as I read Ernaux—and utter
surprise—her specifics are unexpected and the nature of the perceptions
as unified as in that bizarre phenomenon called personality. She is not telling someone else's story. She is not performing anything rehearsed. This is
a sensibility grappling with an occurrence. The grappling, and its way of
becoming distinctive from writer to writer, is of the essence. That kind of
newness will only ever come from a mortal, organic awareness.*

Here is the human version of the telling anomaly. If AlphaGo
made a move that made experts suspect a human capacity, so the writer's original usage, drawn from personal experience, defies what I'm
tempted to call the "machine human." Again, the anomaly can only
emerge from the context of a lived life, the one thing the algorithm
cannot generate. In art, the anomaly is the gate to newness.

I think of Borges' witty play on this issue in his story "Pierre
Menard, Author of the Quixote," in which the eponymous writer sets
out to duplicate Cervantes' classic word by word, by, in effect, becoming Cervantes, experiencing all the things the author had, recreating
the novel by way of his own predictive algorithm: himself. The joke,
of course, is that his exact copy is not Don Quixote. It has everything
except the soul of the original, which emerged from authentic life
experiences, not simulated ones. Does it matter which version a reader
reads? No. Yes. No. Yes. . .

~

Here in The Uncanny Valley, the basis of trust is compromised. I
sometimes feel like I'm an actor in a movie in pursuit of a double
agent. I can't believe anything anyone says it may all be a skillful imper-

sonation, a ruse. How can I be sure this bag is really from Prada? How do I know this writing came from a person? The time is coming when I won't.

Obviously, there are many contexts in which the distinction won't matter much—person or program? But where writing is concerned—literary writing—it matters absolutely, and if it ever ceases to, the game as we've known it will be over, and we will lose so much of what literature offers. I don't mean entertainment here—the pleasures of immersion might be found in different formats—but rather the kinds of meaning we've always gotten from writers: the reason we go *to* writers.

Robert Frost famously asserted "No tears in the writer, no tears in the reader." It's a neat aphorism, but it has also been the core assumption underlying the writer-reader exchange. It grounds that exchange in authenticity, for it rests on the premise that much of our written communication is in some way *felt*; and trusts, too, that the reader can somehow sense when the expression is inauthentic.

I also think of Hemingway, who proposed what is famously called the 'iceberg theory,' where certain intended-but-unsaid content remains under the surface of the story, existing there as a contributing resonance—because the writer felt it. *Only* because. A sophisticated program might emulate the terse Hemingway style and produce a story that makes use of the basic Hemingway themes and his basic structural approach. And a reader might be fooled by it, it's true, but that berg is just a floating wedge of ice with no mass beneath the water. It's a Potemkin iceberg, an emperor togged out in invisible new clothes. The theory, like Frost's assertion, depends entirely on the real emotion existing. A *person* had put those words in place.

~

And now the broader and deeper issues—the ones that so often invite derogatory dismissal when they're raised because as a culture we tend to shy away from earnest inquiry.

Such as: what happens when the basic assumption of human accountability is brought into question, when we are no longer sure if any text, not to mention any assertion, has behind it a legitimate human authority?

We are already experiencing a culture-wide erosion of trust, not only in our public life but in other spheres as well. Boundaries everywhere are becoming murky. Simulation, impersonation, the doctoring of images, online hacks—the causes are many. With so much instability, individuality and independent volition come under considerable pressure. How do we retain a grounded sense of self, a strong 'I,' when so many of our worldly transactions now take place within a vast automated system? The digital interface greets us at every turn, and we find ourselves dealing less and less often with actual people. Pull the lens back. We are so complexly interlinked that once-futuristic scenarios of a hive mind no longer seem that outlandish.

So, how are we to respond? How *can* we? There is no way to go up against a system so overwhelming and anonymous, unreachable. There was once the saying: "You can't fight city hall." And that was when city hall was just city hall. Now it's everything. What's our choice? Do we take Voltaire's advice in *Candide* and look to cultivate our own garden? What would *that* even mean?

~

Everything I've written, from the first, grows from this conviction. The tide of 0s and 1s is washing over all of us, changing so many features of our public landscape, and I can't help but wonder how much all that abstraction is reaching our deeper interior levels. Those levels are where the intensities of contemplation take place—reading and writing and the self-making they foster. They are where we really live, and are now where we have to look to find some basis for hope.

Is this, then, another defense of the book, of reading, writing, and our threatened inwardness? It is. I've made some of these claims before, but the situation is always changing. The impacts of the personal computer were mightily transformative, no one will deny that, and they prepared the way for what we're experiencing now. But what that computing enabled looks like a mere prelude now. AI culture is momentous in ways we can't yet fully grasp.

The digital exists as a near-ubiquitous scrim between person and world. At the same time, because digital technology can out-perform us in almost every sphere, a collective psychological demotion is in progress. If we feel this less than we might, it's because the same technology bombards us with nonstop entertainment. Bright lights, catchy bits. Think of distraction as a kind of Trojan Horse.

There is, of course, the distraction we experience on an immediate and daily level, fragmenting our attention at every turn—a noise in the street, a song on the radio, a ping on our cell-phone. . . But I'm talking about something more consequential, both personal and collective: the distraction from self. It's incremental, and it happens over time. Making our way through our digitized day, ever attuned to the summons coming from all directions, we grow habituated, and are almost not aware of being so.

More distressing still is how we start to find it possible, even easier, to live that way—at a distance from the ever-fainter appeals of the "I." The question becomes whether selfhood can fully exist without inward reflection and the independent exercise of the imagination?

I can't conceive of living without the idea of self-making, and without the trust that the individual life is a movement 'toward,' that it has intent, and that it might in the end hold the possibility of a personal coherence. I believe it's there to be found, even in our fragmented times, unique to everyone and, in Keats' words, "proved upon our pulses."

And What *Is* Writing?

Ah, the old questions, the good questions, the old Heideggerian questions that seem so very basic on the surface, but then you get caught in the implications and realize that they go on and on and that you'll only go crazy trying to answer them. Heidegger liked to ask, "What is thinking?" which ended up being question enough to support a whole philosophy. Me? I've been staying close to my own ground, asking merely, "What is writing?" I'm not looking to found a philosophy, though. In truth, I'm just responding to a short rumination I read online, I forget where, in which the writer went through his day, itemizing his actions, enumerating all the dodges and distractions, finally coming to the conclusion—surprise!—that he usually did very little actual *writing*.

The scenario was distressingly familiar. In fact, it got me thinking that if the actual production of words was what finally qualified one as a "writer," then my title to the vocation could be said to be a bit provisional lately. Where for long years I filled every free crevice of time with the action of words, with pages typed, later word-processed, xeroxed, posted, faxed, FedExed, now, for reasons I have yet to fathom, longer and longer stretches go by without any of that pressurized exertion, but also, strangely, without my feeling that I *need* to be putting words to the page. I just came back from two weeks of travel, weeks which directly followed two weeks spent running a writing residency, and nothing—*nothing*—of value was produced.

Or, rather, nothing of value made it to page or screen. One twelfth of the year has proved a complete blank, so far as generation goes. This would have been unthinkable in former days, or, if thinkable, then not to be endured without the worst mortifications of conscience. But I sit here now feeling only the slightest taint of the old guilt. I am uncontorted by the gut-twist of fraudulence. I would even say that I feel as much a writer as ever before, and I feel it in a way that I did not, quite, in my fullest flow of productivity.

How to explain? If I say—to get Heideggerian again—"the singer *sings*" or "the dancer *dances*," who would venture to dispute me? The action defines the craft, embodies it. There is a distinct line that marks the limit and the origin of the activity. Not-singing bears little or no relation to singing; not dancing bears little or no relation to dancing, or so I say as an outsider. But by contrast there are a great many modes, or states, of not-writing that are closely bound to—are indeed, as philosophers might say, partially *constitutive* of writing. And this has everything to do with the question: "what is writing?" For one thing, it makes the question vexing. For if writing is not defined as the putting of words to a surface, then what is it?

I'm thinking now of the well-known opening sentence of F. Scott Fitzgerald's *The Great Gatsby:* "In my younger and more vulnerable years my father gave me some advice that I've been turning over in my mind ever since." Irresistible prose—it perfectly launches this greatest of novels. We would all agree that during the writing of these words, Fitzgerald was the writer *par excellence*, an intelligence fully in the act of inspired, distilled production. A sentence like this almost never comes flying forth out of nowhere. It embodies a balance, a poise, a precision, a subdued pressure of wisdom, that signals a highly developed verbal sensibility. The person who wrote the sentence was a writer, and if it chanced that he was not one by professed vocation, then at very least he inhabited the true writing mind for the duration of that composition.

But even if the author *was* self-declared as writer, the odds are that the words did not flow effortlessly to the page, but actually got there as a result of some intense labor. Writing, we all know, is not just about end result, the final output; it is also about the process that leads to the result. All attempts at getting the words in their right, inevitable-feeling order must likewise count as writing. In this regard, I often think of Frank Budgen's account of meeting James Joyce on the streets of Zurich and finding the Master quite pleased with himself. Budgen asked him if the work was going well, and Joyce answered that it was indeed: he had given the day to getting the words he had chosen for a particular sentence into the right sequence. He thought he had finally found it. So yes, the moving and adding and deleting of words, no matter how much ground is finally gained—or lost—must be counted as writing.

Here, though, we enter on the slippery slope. For now it is not a very big step to count all verbal manipulations, even aborted ones, as similarly defining the writing act. And if Fitzgerald had spent, say, weeks prior to getting that first sentence right in filling wastebaskets with rejected versions, could he still not be legitimately honored as carrying out the writer's task?

How much does our conception of the vocation require the physical imposition of marks on paper or screen? If our author had sat at his desk and merely thought his way toward that sentence (and, implicitly, the ones that would follow), testing sequences on his ear, rejecting one after another in search of the combination, never once picking up his pen, would his activity be any less writing? Is the act defined more by the physical commitment of words than by the processes that underlie it? I think not. Writing is the manipulation of words toward expressive sense, and a word is no less a word when held in the auditory imagination than when bodied forth in ink. Indeed, if focus is the determinant, it may be even more fully realized in thought than execution. I have, I know, placed many thousands, more likely millions, of words on paper with the barest awareness of their weight or meaning, and I have thought countless others with what felt like the purest clarity.

I'll take another step now and say that I don't think that a writer has to be sitting at his desk at all to be considered "in the act"— one's physical situation is a mere formality. The same verbal testing processes can be undertaken while one is lying on one's back on the lawn or pacing slowly up and down in front of the corner delicatessen.

You can see what I'm getting at here. Writing shades into thinking about writing in ways that are hard to pinpoint, but this thinking has to be seen as an essential part of the process. Why? Because the process cannot take place without it. Writing is the fulfillment of an action, a dynamic, that begins in observation or thought; it is the emergence of the original stimulus into artistic self-consciousness, experience as packaged by the writer to be received by the sensibility of an eventual reader.

It is a complex and elusive business. This more purposeful, targeted thinking-toward-writing that I'm considering does not arise from nothing. How could it? The mental movement that directly feeds the production of literary work is rooted in the broader life of thought itself, and to write a sentence Fitzgerald or Welty or Baldwin or any other achieved writer might create requires a seedbed, a long-established practice of observation and reflection, and a particular kind of thinking about the ways of the world, about people, about everything that forms the "stuff" of the art, which is to say—for nothing is alien to writing—that it requires a good deal of thinking about anything at all. It is the particular nature of that thinking that counts.

This last distinction is crucial. For it cannot be that anyone thinking about anything qualifies as a writer. That would generalize the concept of writing into utter absurdity. I have in mind here only the thinking that might eventuate in writing—thinking carried out by those who filter their experience with that end in mind. But isn't this a circular situation? Am I not saying that only thinking by writers qualifies? We are back to the original question. *Who* is the writer? The writer is one who writes, of course. But the writer must also in a preliminary way be defined as one who processes his or her experience in order to write about it. The chicken, the egg; the chicken, the egg. I wouldn't bring any of this gnarly business up at all if it were not for this question of self-validation—my looking for a way to establish in good conscience that I am a writer even if I am not writing. This conscience, I will emphasize, is mine alone. Though I grant that the aim of writing is to reach others, I don't in this one regard care much whether others think I am doing the work or not. I just want to be square with myself. The idea of being a writer is what stamps my ticket; it is the one thing that I feel redeems my experiences from mere contingency. By this I mean that relating to one's life under the assumption that it is all potentially material to be shaped into artistic expression is completely unlike going through the identical experiences without that assumption. For me it is the difference between meaning and meaninglessness—and a greater difference cannot be imagined between any two terms.

I have long admired Jorge Luis Borges' little *ficción* "Pierre Menard, Author of the Quixote," but these reflections have me thinking that I've only partially understood it. The story, familiar to many readers, recounts one Pierre Menard's attempt to recreate Cervantes' *Don Quixote* word for word without reference to the original. Menard sets out to assimilate (so far as possible) the same influences and experiences. He wants to re-invent the work afresh in identical form by, in effect, *becoming* the author. In this he both succeeds (partially) and—illuminatingly—fails. I always believed that Borges was writing a kind of parable about originality, about how an author quite literally "holds title" to a work of imagination, and how the meanings of all statements are contingent on context and the slippery business of intention.

Certainly Borges' work suggests these ideas, but to take them as primary also misses a deeper wisdom in the tale, which I see now is an investigation of the core essence of authorship. "Pierre Menard" studies the very relation between self and the materials—experiences—that are subject to creative transformation. What, exactly, comprises narrative, and on what terms? The interesting—telling—aspect of Borges' patently absurd imagining (we accept it as a metaphysical ploy) is found in the distinction between Cervantes' and Menard's experiences. For Cervantes—this is primary—readings and life-encounters and thoughts sparked in him, via unknowable alchemy, the artistic aspiration, the will, and then—only then—became the material that would be transformed into story.

Menard, on the other hand, is already artistically predisposed; he is besotted with the desire to produce a masterpiece. He looks to the readings and re-stages life encounters to make himself into the author who would produce, exactly, the *Quixote*. Menard's approach is result-oriented, determined, deterministic, whereas Cervantes' had been open-ended, like that of any person living the unknown, unknowable life. Borges' "Menard," then, is about willing the sensibility to fashion given materials into what would appear on the page as inevitable narrative expressions. The parable is less occupied with imaginative origination and more with the idea that a true writerly response to a set of givens will yield the desired work. It puts the burden of the writer's activity not on the actual production of words, but on the inward sifting and shaping of experience that eventually calls that work forth. The creative act of writing feels secondary to the achieving of the desired sensibility.

I pursue this whimsy because it supports my contention that writing is understood and defined not by the obvious placing of words on the page, and not even by the specific thoughts and inner processes that lead directly to that; rather, it is a condition, a disposition that considers experience in a certain way, whether or not that consideration results in output. The writer is one who experiences the world in ways that could, under fortuitous circumstances, result in verbal expression. Being a writer is filtering all experience through a scrim of potential verbal significance. *Potential.* It is, in other words, living liminally, hovering at all times at the threshold of transformation, the place where language comes alive.

I remember how, even when I was very young, I felt the thrall, the seduction, of this state, not just the making things from words, but preliminary to that, and no less important, the transformative orientation toward experience. I could not say what it was—I still can't—but I was sure that I recognized it when I saw it. In certain readers I observed, for instance. Something of what I think of now as the writerly stance, the ongoing filtering of experience, was often perceptible in the reader's demeanor, manifesting itself in what was to me a deeply attractive quality of absence, of not being fully present to the moment, which I interpreted not as a failure so much as evidence of partial attendance at some infinitely more interesting event. This was for me the first glimmer of the writing life, and I have to say that while much has worn away from my fantasies of what that life might be like—certainly on the public, worldly front—my attraction to the feeling of that absence, my pull toward the conjectural, toward something just registered in intuition and open to meanings, remains undiminished. That ongoing awareness has gradually changed my attitude toward writing, which I now regard a bit less as the doing and more and more as the inhabiting of a state that might, but also might *not*, finally certify itself in a procession of words on a page.

(2009)

The Nightcrawler, Joan Miró

I was deep inside the hollow of an MRI machine at Mount Auburn Hospital a few weeks ago, laid out face-up in my johnny in a very narrow groove, my head positioned in a separate socket of sorts, with a kind of goalie-mask appliance clipped down over it so that I couldn't see much of anything, and with earplugs in my ears and protective pads inserted to cushion the sides of my head. I'd been given a wired-up bulb to hold, something a game-show contestant might have, and told to squeeze it if I needed help or attention, and then the technician pushed the whole luge like conveyance on its rail into the tubular aperture and the forty-some minute madness of beeps, clicks, and buzzings began.

I was in that hollow tube because I had quite suddenly lost hearing in my right ear, and with it my normal sense of balance. It happened the night before what was to be the start of our summer vacation to a lake in Vermont. I waited the night to see if it might go away. It didn't. The computer said: could be serious, see a doctor. But it was the weekend. My doctor was off-duty, there was only the ER, which felt dire. Better safe than sorry, I thought. There was a great long waiting in a "quiet" room. When he finally came, the doctor couldn't find anything, but he wanted to rule out stroke or tumor. I had never been in one of these machines before. People who had (including my wife) said they were loud, claustrophobia-inducing, an ordeal. I didn't know how I would react, and I had no idea of how I would pass the time.

What *does* one do inside a racketing cylinder for the better part of an hour? One thinks, or else one tries not to think. I went with the former, not knowing how to succeed at the other. I could almost feel the anxious mind looking for its hand-hold. Mercifully, one offered itself. Now, looking back, I will attest that it was Julio Cortázar—my unexpected thoughts of him—that saved the occasion. Cortázar, and, yes, the fact that the MRI found nothing, and that after some hours the deafness resolved itself . . .

Julio Cortázar. Here follows another of those chains of author-and-book-related associations that I can't seem to not write, and that therefore I feel I need not apologize for writing. And truly, why apologize? Such narratives have to be one of the more reliable ways that the writing mind can be observed—the recorded trail of thoughts and impressions, possibly not unlike that left by the contrast dye I'd just had injected so that the radiologists could read my inner workings.

It had been a true literary romance, Cortázar's and mine, a writer-reader connection that sent out its first electricity one afternoon forty years ago when I was crouched on my knees shelving books. I was, at the time, just out of college, working my first real job at the recently opened Borders in Ann Arbor. I was the standard-issue book besotted twenty-something. My knees did not yet crack like they do now. I was putting away fiction, down in the Cs. The book in my hand was something called *Hopscotch*—a black Plume trade paperback, I remember. And I did what I so often did. I opened to the first page and said (in my thoughts) my own version of what the Russian impresario Diaghilev supposedly said to young Vaslav Nijinsky: "Astonish me!" How few of the novels finally did. But on this occasion I read:

Would I find La Maga? Most of the time it was just a case of my putting in an appearance, going along the Rue de la Seine to the arch leading into the Quai de Conti, and I would see her slender form against the olive-ashen light which floats along the river as she crossed back and forth on the Pont Des Arts, or leaned over the iron rail looking at the water.

The opening got me right away—this was, if not where I lived, then everywhere I *wanted* to live. Here, in two sentences, compressed in a way that I'm still trying to unpack, were so many of the constituents of the young man's romance with the world—which is to say his imagining of his own future. A mysterious woman (La Maga, the name suggesting magic, the mages . . .); a setting that was beyond irresistible to a suburb-bred American boy—Paris, the Seine, trysting place of all the tormented and desperate ones; a logic of encounter that relied on serendipity, the finding of the other all bound up with fatedness; and of course the imagery, the writing, even as translated: that "olive-ashen light," La Maga's leaning over "the iron rail looking at the water."

I took *Hopscotch* home that night and let it become what used to be called a *vade mecum*—my guide, my "handbook for consultation." Those first sentences had made me think the novel would be existential, bohemian, prose in the key of Henry Miller or Lawrence Durrell, both writers I loved back then. But I was wrong. It *was* those things, true—very romantic, very bohemian—but it was something very much else as well. For Cortázar had devised a fascinating structural ploy that allowed him to mimic, or enact, the appealingly casual progress of a group of expatriates living in a chance world. He divided the book in half—the first part being chapters of narrative, and the second comprising a compendium of quotations, asides, alternate scenes. Every section, whether narrative or from the compendium, had at the end a number in parenthesis, a suggestion for the next chapter or section the reader might go to.

The author suggested that there were three ways in which the novel could be read. One was the old-style consecutive way, another was by following the hopscotching pattern marked out by the numbers, and the third, most radical, was completely arbitrary: open at any point and read, then open elsewhere. That the author would think this was a viable option was, in the phrase *du jour*, "mind-blowing" to me. This *Hopscotch* was not just a novel, absolutely not, it was a philosophy, a manifesto about how we live (or might live) in the world. It was zen, jazz, beat improvisation, Dada/surrealism, OULIPO, situationism, all rolled into one.

Reading, I found that the basic narrative circumstance, the Paris-based romance between the characters Horacio and La Maga, though absorbing, was finally less compelling to me than everything else in the package, including the package. Because Cortázar, an Argentine expatriate who had won his early praise from Borges himself, was an artificer and referencer of great capacity. In truth, it was by living with this novel, reading it this way and that, hunting along its many paths, looking up the writers and thinkers he quoted, that I started on my secondary education, one I now consider to have been as formative as my more official schooling. If the official schooling can be whimsically likened to reading the novel from the first chapter forward, then the counter-education, or parallel-education, would be the Cortázarian process, letting one thing take you to another, following threads willy-nilly as they cross and re-cross, creating their cat's cradle of suppositions (the cat's cradle being, along with hopscotch itself, one of the author's favorite images, with its underlying suggestion that games are complex psychological architectures, and that nothing is so serious as a child's purposeful play).

It was through references in *Hopscotch* that I first got wind of Malcolm Lowry and Robert Musil, both of whom would become great spirit-masters, and Claude Lévi-Strauss, whose *Tristes Tropiques* became a doorway into the whole then-contemporary and very urgent-seeming Structuralism debate. Such string-ends were everywhere. I had only to pick one. Georges Bataille, Antonin Artaud, Witold Gombrowicz, Octavio Paz, Kazimir Malevich, Meister Eckhart, Werner Heisenberg, Lawrence Durrell, Heraclitus, René Char—can I stop now? "Heady" is the adjective, admittedly clichéd, I would apply to the experience of having all these literary encounters right at the moment of intellectual readiness, while working in a bookstore, no less.

Writers and references are, of course, always everywhere—the world abounds in potential connections—but at that point in my life, to become a true reading incentive, a name or a book needed to be certified for me; it had to pass through the magnetic field of the sensibility of some admired other. Which is exactly what was happening to me as I read. I filled my notebooks with quotes and attributions. Once a name or a title had been flagged by Cortázar, seen as important by him, it signified. I could set out to look for it.

This kind of pursuit of recommendations is, I'm thinking, the 180-degree opposite of having titles, films, or songs offered up by some Pandora-type algorithm, as was the manner of the pursuit itself. No Wikipedia or Amazon: the Cortázarian searches moved the real body through real space, from bookstore to bookstore, almost echoing how his number system invited the reader to move back and forth inside the newly reconfigured dimensionality of the novel.

This, my second education, was helped along by the fact that Ann Arbor in those days was one of the book meccas of this country. That tracing of Cortázarian threads went on for some years, right along with all of the flying leaps I was taking at writing fiction of my own. Cortázar was not just a writer I read, he was a writer I aspired to be like—not that I thought it could ever happen. But I loved the image of the man, and I sought it for myself. I tracked down and read the books, they led me to those other heroes, and all the while I wrote my Cortázarian pastiches—such was my fealty—which became only by slow degrees less pastiches and more distinctly expressions that I could call my own (though even as I write now, forty years later, I notice a certain extension-ladder quality in the structure of certain sentences, like this one, which clearly owes a good deal to that early obsessive reading).

Cortázar's influence continued for some years, but then gradually, for a host of reasons, one of which was the example of so many of those "discovered" writers, it started to fade. His books (the story collections, the novels, the wonderful miscellanies like his *Cronopios and Famas*) stayed in a prominent place on the shelves, of course. But, as happens, years would go by without any of them being opened. These gaps come and they are strange. But in my defense—and also addressing the spirit of my mentor—I would say that the books felt so familiar, so *ingested*, that they did not need that attention.

Years, then decades passed, and *that's* strange to contemplate, too, that larger increment, but I'll leave it for another time. Though Cortázar has never been quite absent from my peripheral vision, he was not full-focus present, not anymore. Not until the other day, that is, when I found myself strapped to a rolling luge and inserted deep into the maw of a magnetic chamber. And suddenly there I was, holding the idea of my old master Cortázar like the end of a string attached to something that would lift me out of the clicking and buzzing assaulting me from all sides.

How did this happen? Well, in a Cortázarian manner, I'm pleased to say. By which I mean: through the sly but traceable back-channels of serendipity. For in the days before our scheduled vacation departure, while with one part of my brain I was pondering what books to bring along (full of the hope that the idle days would restore some capacity for real reading), with the other I was clearing the desk at *AGNI*, working through a pile of promising submissions.

One of these was a fetchingly off-beat meditation on the idea of collage, and early in the piece the writer referred to a book by Cortázar that I'd never heard of: *Save Twilight*. I stopped, took pause. Could it be? A Cortázar I knew not? A quick Amazon search revealed it was a small book in the City Lights Pocket Poets series. An incidental book, I thought. *Not necessarily incidental at all*, I corrected myself. I made a mental note to order it and read on.

Ever since I first started reading seriously, I've been convinced that whatever has to rivulet its way into my psyche, will. The need is determined by some inner divination, not purposeful thought. That idea or image or reference becomes part of the saturation of my inner life, and thus might impinge on my thinking at any point—though, of course, such impinging happens most reliably when there is some occasion, some readiness. It did not take long in this case. When I got home from work that afternoon, I found myself going straight to the shelves in the living room and looking at my clutch of Cortázar books. *62: A Model Kit, End of the Game, All Fires the Fire, We Love Glenda So Much, Cronopios and Famas, Hopscotch* . . . It was clear: I would have to bring something by Cortázar along to the lake . . .

~

And here it is, in hand. There is no anticipating what might happen when a book, the right or the provocative book, enters the stream of days. After some protracted dipping, sampling passages, I finally settled on a book I'd not read called *Around the Day in Eighty Worlds*. I've had the thing forever and have never known what to make of it. Not novel or stories, not quite a book of essays, *Eighty Worlds* is a creative miscellany, a book that seems to explain itself as it makes itself: an idiosyncratic daybook comprising an array of nonsequential meditations.

Nonsequential, yes, but not arbitrary either. This is, I have every faith, a book on a thematic mission. I have sensed as much through all these years of owning and never reading it. A book of serious play. A book that, now that I *have* begun to read in it, proposes a very eccentric imagining of alternative modes of living. No big surprise here. It was, after all, some recognition of this very quality that first drew me to Cortázar's prose, a quality already obvious in those opening sentences of *Hopscotch*.

Reading the right book, the right author, at the right time, can still, if less often than in younger days, put me inside a force field that is unlike anything else I know. How to account for the roiling together of memory and the imagined future? How is it that I carry the humming vibration of my reading all through my days, or in certain passages feel the membrane become so thin that I feel I can almost touch the soul of the writer? The business is more uncanny still when the author is writing about just such mysteries himself.

Eighty Worlds is not conducive to the usual style of vacation reading, which involves lying back and getting inveigled into some cunning narrative, all burdensome disbelief suspended for an extended interval—that being, in truth, the ideal of vacationing. *Eighty Worlds* is not a book to be approached thus. Rather, it is a work that, as Cortázar himself writes of his beloved José Lezama Lima's *Paradiso*, "isn't read; it is consulted, you move through it line by line, essence by essence...." A philosopher of chance, the author has used chance to construct a work that is in large part *about* chance. A kind of chance decided me on taking it along on vacation, and in the sidelong manner of chance I feel it entering my time here—my days and, differently, my nights.

A word or two on this empirically contested business, for there is chance and chance. There is the lay common-sense version, which basically asserts that inevitably in the welter of events come juxtapositions and concurrences that seem significant, that cause the onlooker to shake her head and marvel. And then there is the other, more philosophically-charged version, which has been a subject of intense interest to Surrealists, Buddhists, Jungians, and, of course, Cortázar himself.

This view holds that we have, most of us, boxed ourselves into a certain way of living, assuming that our explanatory structures give us an adequate picture of the world, which we then call the truth, or the way of things. We are, Cortázar might say, moving through a vast teeming darkness with just the cone of flashlight illumination in front of us. We imagine we have the all of it, when in fact it's quite the reverse. We have nothing, only the illusion of knowing. Cortázar's "chance," whimsical and profound, stands for all that is not comprehended in our Western-rationalist-bourgeois outlook. It assumes the porousness of boundaries, the connection of dispersed events through perceived and sensed meaning; it proposes significances of resemblance and selective abolition of rigidly sequential time-frames; it feels everywhere soaked through by the irreality of the unconscious.

It came clear as I started that I had brought not just a book but also a vision of things with me up to the piney lake in Vermont. And so, instead of sitting back and immersing myself in another familiar narrative premise, I found myself carefully circling this now-almost talismanic object that had been sitting on my shelves for many years. I wanted to activate it. It made me a bit nervous, but I knew that I wanted to release Cortázar's thoughts into my thoughts, to have them influence the momentum and direction. This may seem no big thing on the glib face of things, but, if you believe that we are as we think, it can be life-changing. Maybe I'm being slightly dramatic in saying this. For it's usually not a matter of any one insight or expression having that kind of thrust. But a series of insights and expressions, making an atmosphere, creating an outlook—*this* can have an effect.

So for days I nibbled. I would pick up the book and read twenty pages, then set it down again. I was not reading with a pencil in hand—this was my vacation, after all—but whenever I hit a particularly striking passage, I would fold down the corner, the size of the earmark suggesting just how important I felt it to be.

A sampler of dog-eared passages:

Much of what I have written falls into the category of eccentricity, because I have never admitted a clear distinction between living and writing; if in my life I have managed to disguise an only partial participation in my circumstances, I still cannot deny that eccentricity in what I write, since I write because I am only half there or not there at all.

On the incidental perception of beauty:

I have just seen a duck on the lake in the Bois de Boulogne, and it possessed such a marvelous beauty that I had to stop and sit down by the side of the lake for I don't know how long, admiring its grace, the insolent joy in its eyes, that delicate double line carved by its breast in the surface of the water, which gradually widened until it disappeared in the distance. My enthusiasm was not just aroused by the duck but came from something that was given material form in it, that might also appear in a dead leaf balanced on the edge of the bank, or in an orange crane, enormous and delicate, framed against the blue evening sky, or in the smell of a train car as you enter with a ticket for a trip of several hours when everything will rush by, stations, a ham sandwich . . . : all of this seems to me so beautiful, so nearly impossible, that to have it there within my reach fills me with a kind of inner sauce, so deliciously green that I never want to come to the end of it.

And:

I recall a curious quotation from, I think, Roger Fry: a precocious child who was talented at drawing explained his method of composition by saying, "First I think and then I draw a line around my think." In the case of my stories, it is the exact opposite: the verbal line that will draw them is started without any prior "think"; it is like a coagulation, raw material that is already taking shape in the story, that is perfectly clear even though it might seem that nothing could be more confused; in this it is like the inverted signs of the dream—we have all had dreams of midday clarity that became formless shapes, meaningless masses, when we awoke. Do you dream while you are awake when you write a short story? . . . But while the analogy is obvious, the relationship is inverted, at least in my case, because I begin with the shapeless mass and write something that only then becomes a coherent and valid story per se.

I could keep going, but I find that writers who quote too much from other writers start to get irritating, never mind how good the quotes. I'm citing these passages to make my point about the kind of thinking, the nature of the worldview, that was impinging on my own. It is impossible to read Cortázar, for me anyway, and not be aware of a certain steady pressure on what I consider my way of seeing things.

Just moments ago, to take a single instance from what have been many in these last days, I interrupted my typing of these passages and got up. I had to get something from the adjacent bunkhouse building. It had been raining much of the night. Walking along the open but covered walkway, caught up in the distracted mood that overtakes me when I write, I nonetheless noticed, in that way of peripheral noticing, the most fantastic—elegant—looping design on the wet boards at my feet. "Someone here has dropped a string," I thought, and I was already marveling at the fantastic shape an accident can make, when I slowed my step and looked closer. I saw that it was not a string at all. This striking free-form Miró sketch at my feet was in fact the wet trail left by the movement of a very long earthworm—nightcrawler—that was, at that very moment, itself the moving front part of the line: pink, pasty-textured, fully extended, the engineer of the train behind him.

I had, you see, just copied out the passage about the duck, the delicate double line it left in the water, and because of that, but also *not*—because I like to think that this is the kind of thing that would strike me in any case—I had to stop for a moment of pure beholding: first of the sight, the beauty of the trail, then the anomalousness of its maker, somehow unseemly, too pinkly naked, in the gray morning light . . . And then, and then . . . Still paused there, leaning over, I could not ignore the obvious connection to everything I'd been thinking and writing. Which then brought on a kind of secondary marveling, one that wrapped itself around the first, and had the larger effect of energizing me to go back to my writing. As if only thus, through the ever-mysterious agencies of syntax, seemingly disparate things could be gathered together into some sensible expression.

I marked the insistent circularity of it all and felt I caught the deeper sense of Cortázar's observation about the lack of distinction between his reading and writing. Chance was somehow in the air, and it recalled to me, as I returned from the bunkhouse and passed the slow train again, the afternoon just days ago when I was prone inside that MRI cylinder, when the thoughts of Cortázar had first come to me. What I saw now was that they had come not just willy-nilly, or because a reference in an essay put him in my thoughts, but because, in Cortázarian fashion, I was somehow already onto some next inner phase, thinking *toward* it in ways that writing would have to reveal to me. It was then, as if in confirmation, I remembered one other marked-out place, the one with the biggest dog-ear fold of all.

In a chapter, one of his eighty "worlds," called "The Broken Doll," Cortázar ruminates on the writing of *Hopscotch* and the place in it of this kind of chance. "We know," he writes, "that attention acts as a lightning rod. Merely by concentrating on something one causes endless analogies to collect around it, even to penetrate the boundaries of the subject itself: an experience that we call coincidence, serendipity—the terminology is extensive." I had to read it over and over, for it is a literally fabulous conception. On several levels. First, that the act of attention *invites* analogy—that it is not just a heightened beholding, but an active agency: the ramifications for writing are enormous. And, second, that a strong enough concentration can affect the thing concentrated on, blurring, in effect, the traditional perceiver/perceived distinction. This, too, bears further contemplating.

But Cortázar goes on, articulating a kind of philosophy of the creative act, at least his as he was writing *Hopscotch*. "My experience," he writes,

> *has been that in these circular travels what is really significant surrounds a central absence, an absence that, paradoxically, is the text being written or to be written. In the years when I was working on Hopscotch, this saturation reached the point where the only legitimate response was to accept without comment the meteor shower that came through the windows of streets, books, conversations, and everyday circumstances and to convert them into the passages, fragments, and required or optional chapters of the other that formed around an ill-defined story of searches and missed encounters. . . .*

There. I said I would not quote more, but this last is a kind of keystone for the imagined arch formed by the others. It proposes the idea that between the writer's consciousness and his circumstance there moves a two-way traffic, as if the work-to-be makes itself through the medium of the writer. The notion is somewhat different from both the ancient idea of the Muse offering dictation and the opposing conception that one *has* an idea and then makes it real, like the precocious child drawing the line around his "think." For me it reverberates a recognition that I have had again and again—that on the best occasions the expression mysteriously exceeds the felt capacities of the writer, that we are in certain ways a good deal smarter than we know ourselves to be. The shortfall that constitutes our normal self—the "I" going about its business—is unfortunate. Would that we could always be as alert and insightful as we sometimes are. But, then, if we could, the writer, the artist, would be out of a job.

(2014)

The Fitful Tracing of a Portal

Back in the early nineteenth century, Stendhal made a now-famous assertion. The novel, he wrote, "is a mirror carried along a high road. At one moment it reflects to your vision the azure skies, at another the mire of the puddles at your feet. And the man who carries this mirror in his pack will be accused by you of being immoral! His mirror shows the mire, and you blame the mirror! Rather blame that high road upon which the puddle lies, still more the inspector of roads who allows the water to gather and the puddle to form."

For two centuries, this has been a central understanding of the novel: that it is a reflection, not always literal, of the world we live in, presenting what the writer sees. It is also, of course, a construction, a constraint in the sense of being a kind of container, finite; it is a reality unto itself which nevertheless informs on our common reality. There are structural and thematic exceptions everywhere, naturally, experiments of every description, but they mostly work within the boundaries and, by and large, accept the assumptions of that common reality. To date, the novel has occupied itself mainly with the analog. I've wondered for a long time when that might start to change.

Some years ago, reflecting on the outlook for fiction—the novel in particular—I found myself posing a most basic question: If the stuff of the novel has always had our material reality as an implicit

referent—the basis of its actions, circumstances, conflicts, and aspirations, each reflected in a carried mirror—then what happens when
that reality changes?

Simply: our waking lives comprise less and less that can be readily portrayed. Most of us now spend a great deal of time in a shared
reality largely comprising the intangible processes of the digital and
virtual. I was worrying about this long before Covid struck. But when
it did come, the pandemic put pressure on everything, thrusting us
into isolated bubbles and forcing millions of us to rely on digital
makeshifts. Suddenly, routine parts of our former lives could happen
entirely from the "comfort" of home. Attending or presenting classes,
shopping at the nearest food store, conferring with one-time offi-
cemates. New needs expanded and intensified the screen life we
already had.

An unabashed techno-skeptic, I came face to face in these months
with my biggest *abstract* fear: that this thrust into collective digital life
would confirm the viability of more broad based screen interactions.
It would thus further accelerate an already accelerating transformation—the great shift from a primarily analog to a primarily virtual
engagement with the world.

I've been thinking about this in literary terms, too, most recently
through a particular strain of fiction that's in the news lately. This
strain is as yet a tentative new expression, a blip in the ongoing, but
given the transition that we're working through now, it seems relevant
and suggestive in the extreme. The specific provocation is a novel
that—canary/coalmine—is being assessed as a possible next step
for the genre.

~

Patricia Lockwood's novel *No One Is Talking About This* is presented in
two parts, the first a rolling compendium of tweets of every description, meant to evoke the sensations and compulsions of online experi-

ence; the second a genuine off-screen family emergency that compels the narrator to step away from what she calls the "portal" and take action in a world that has in many ways become distant for her. This sudden break allows her to start questioning the value and reach of her dominantly virtual life. She does not, in the end, make the yes/no call of rejecting the internet. Life is no longer that simple.

Lockwood's book suggests several ways of considering the potential impact of our cyber existence on the writing and reading of the novel. If a novelist is still carrying a mirror along the road, showing different aspects of her own times, less is being reflected. How to show what we do and who we are? The glass gives back mainly more glass: people fixated on a bright rectangle, typing and sending messages, arranging their fiscal lives, or consuming pornography. Can Nolan and Jasmine be characters a reader connects with if the main business of their lives happens within Lockwood's "portal"? The powerful conditioning of that vortex is not easily ignored, even if circumstances outside the portal continue to be part of their daily living.

I'm not talking here about the more familiar kind of fiction—the traditional model, still dominant, that presents the way we live, only without the digital interface. That mode will remain prominent so long as the reading public asks for it, I suppose, but at some point it will feel quaint.

As for fiction that does want to contend with our new reality, what are the options? Ambitious writers will find their own answers, of course, but a big part of their effort will be in determining how—whether by coming up with strategies to make on-screen activity vivid, or by finding work-arounds that allow characters to interact primarily in the old "real" world: the vacation where devices are left behind, the week spent marooned without battery power…

For the writer working to catch hold of now, there is the option, which Lockwood pursues, of plunging the reader into the virtual, and letting the presence of that reality become a distinct plot element, its impact part of the exploration. But that is the greatest of challenges. For reproducing internet activity on the page or screen, whether by writing tweets or somehow incorporating the back-and forth dynamic of links, might very well call forth in the reader the scanning reflexes that the internet has already instilled.

While these reflexes are useful in their way, they are not at all the reflexes we've traditionally employed when reading fiction; they deny the reader any sort of sustained immersion. Is there room for new expression that invites new kinds of engagement and puts no premium on that kind of immersion? Surely there is, or will be, but at that point are we still in the realm of the novel?

The world has changed, the world to be represented has changed, and the reader encountering that representation has changed also. As I contemplate the possibilities of taking the internet-world as subject matter, and addressing the work to an internet-savvy readership, I am also contemplating the bounds of genre.

The literary novel has over the centuries accepted its outliers— *The Life and Opinions of Tristram Shandy, Gentleman, Finnegans Wake, Hopscotch*—while mainly organizing itself around certain norms that we all recognize: characters, plot, scene-based exposition, conflict, and resolution. But those norms, subject to pressures from the growing dominance of digital/virtual culture, are coming to seem increasingly arbitrary.

This, let's remember, is not some sudden new instability. The novel—indeed literature and all the arts—went through a major shake-up a few decades back, the beginnings of what seemed a Nietzschean transvaluation of values. Postmodernism questioned most of our embedded cultural assumptions. Here was a concerted attack on the idea of hierarchy, of Western centrality, of drawn distinctions between high and low—in short, the core principles of the canon. Ideas of originality, imitation, and appropriation were all contested. Former verities were shown to be constructs, not ineluctable givens, and before long the rigidities of the cultural system could be felt to be loosening. That loosening has continued.

But the Lockwood question has a different pitch to it, for Postmodernism happened without the massive momentum of the internet as we have come to know it—the internet which has effected a full-on transformation of our ways of living, creating a culture of "up-for-grabs."

All of this puts genre itself in doubt. What is it and what does it serve? Is the idea of genre something we've devised, or is it a set of natural formations reflecting the inherent nature of a particular kind of expression? Do we have poetry because, as the division of the Muses might suggest, poetry is an order unto itself serving under Erato, obeying different principles from other kinds of verbal expression? A key question, and I'm not sure of the answer. I will say that while reading submissions I find a growing number of poets straying toward expressive options formerly reserved to prose.

The blur is common now, but I am old enough to remember serious debates about the status and admissibility of so-called prose poetry. Which was it—prose or poetry? The distinction exercised people, who often argued tautologically that poetry is poetry. Meanwhile, nonfiction has not just incorporated the use of formerly fictional techniques, but it has also added a category called creative nonfiction, which means that an essay is open to structural innovation as well as a lyric expression that presses hard against the "non" of its label. In fiction, we now have the variant form known as autofiction, which tunnels from the opposite side of the mountain, infusing personal narrative with a fictional dynamic so that the reader at some level wavers between accepting events as really having happened and considering at every moment the possibility that they did not.

Again: whence genre, why genre?

Etymologies are almost always instructive. With a Google search I discover that genre and gender, from early nineteenth century French, are close kin, both expressing the idea of difference. In the case of gender, we are seeing once-assumed differences collapsing, spawning a more nuanced array of designations no longer pledged to neat binaries. So too with genre, where the concept of difference has become shaded, graded, loosened, to accommodate what were formerly transgressive—now viewed as exploratory—energies. Cross-pollination is part of the order of things, with experimental forays becoming what I'm tempted to call sub-genres, but which by now are really their own thing.

Decades ago, a former bookstore employee myself, I remarked on the proliferation of bookstore sections—new signage, nomenclature: Fiction, Genre Fiction (ha), Graphic Novels, Fantasy, Noir . . . Readers were directed to the niche of their choice. This had partly to do with marketing, of course, and we can see versions of the trend across the commercial board. Try going to CVS to buy a tube of toothpaste. There is no such thing as a tube of toothpaste.

But marketing decisions are not ultimately responsible. They mirror in their fashion the transformations happening in society. The internet, the major force here, has become an affinity machine, a means for the like-minded to find one another. Where there are groups, there too will differences announce themselves: sects, enclaves, tribes, parties, pods.

Splintering to this atomized extent is not only new, it is defining. Or, better, redefining, creating by degrees new conceptions on every front. As long-held assumptions of hierarchy are pulled down, the arts are embracing, or purporting to embrace, all manner of new cultural expression. With so many tendencies pushing toward multiplicity, it's hard to see how the very notion of genre won't have to surrender its fixities, and eventually even dissolve.

Thinking a few decades down the road, assuming the expanded dominance of digital interaction, along with the inevitable rewiring of our attention spans and cognitive aptitudes, current divisions are not likely to stay in place. What will it mean to label something "fiction" when more and more writing comes at us in fragments, as pastiche, appropriations, collaborations, autofictions? Very little. And this will surely hold true for the other genres.

It's worth asking what such an erosion of fixed distinctions will bring with it. Catholicity, diversity, and fluidity will be positives, along with a premium placed on voice over plot or narrative consistency. The sacrifice? Here we need to consider our ideas of boundary and limit and the value of constraint. There are those who believe that certain kinds of basic strictures challenge and energize the imagination. I think of Robert Frost, who said that letting go of formal meter was like playing tennis without a net. He was wrong. Free verse flourished beautifully in what then seemed the new permissiveness. What happened was that the aesthetic focus changed, was directed more toward word sounds, line-breaks, and the authority of voice. The loss had to be somehow compensated.

In the initial stages of a transformation, there is fission. Energies are released. There is a sense that freedom is nigh. I felt it back in the sixties, that culture-wide rush of liberation. Rejoicing at new aesthetic possibilities was and is proper.

But—and the great rule of life is that there is always a *but*—balance asks for eventual redress. Freedom is heady; it is also terrifying. I think of Dostoevsky's Grand Inquisitor addressing Jesus in *The Brothers Karamazov*: "Man is tormented by no greater anxiety than to find someone quickly to whom he can hand over that great gift of freedom with which the ill-fated creature is born."

Reviewing Lockwood's novel in *The New York Times*, Merve Emre writes: "one test of the novel in the age of the internet is if it offers enough resistance, on the level of plot or character, structure or tone, to the very media forms it wants to represent. A good novel would not speak in the voice of the internet; it would speak over it, and the clamor it made would allow its critics to hazard a stronger claim for the value of the novel to our virtual lives."

I agree. The writer carrying the mirror down the road of the internet is not the writer making his way down Stendhal's road. To reflect the unbounded, even if only to try to convey the feeling of moving about in the midst of the unbounded, is futile. Mimesis is only suited to those things which have form and edges, that offer purchase. This is what I take Emre to mean by "resistance."

So it's fair to ask how, even allowing for the myriad options of genre fluidity, a writer represents or embodies the world of their experience, when that experience is so dominated by the virtual event. Is the novel in any of its familiar guises adequate? Does it make sense for ambitious writers to work from the former blueprints, given how difficult it is to create the terms for resonant drama or plausible character? If the old-school novel is to carry on as a viable genre, it needs to rise to that challenge. If it can't, it might have to let video, performance, and new un-genred expressions do the job.

But, as we know, most such transitions happen gradually. And to some extent they can be seen to follow the change that comes as generations gradually succeed one another. Think of it. The young are all digitally savvy, able to maneuver the internet with an ease I can't begin to contemplate. They have trained themselves, or been conditioned, to process information and screen-transitions. And while many of us can't keep up with the pace, many of them find it hard to slow their gait enough to stay with the old-school prose narrative.

This is not to assert that literary writing as we know it will no longer exist, or that readers will all have migrated away. Inevitably, new talents will find ways to present their world to them in terms they can relate to. But odds are that that work will have a different status. Insofar as genres will still exist, I suspect they'll depend on the more traditional survivals, while for many they will feel vestigial, like the entries in *Debrett's Handbook* which set out correct social form and protocol for the British upper classes, the dukes, duchesses, and lords.

(2021)

Losing, Finding, Improvising

I find myself thinking a lot about memory these days. It's a subject as vast as consciousness itself, so naturally there are many angles of access. One of these has to do with losing and finding. Not in the literal, object-related sense, but there is a correlation. In the outer world things can be truly lost. A house key might fall from your pocket when you are walking down the street and never be seen again. Or it can be misplaced but then eventually found. Misplacing is different from losing, and here we see how outer and inner connect. Misplacement is either a result of inattention, when the mind is "somewhere else," or a matter of just plain forgetting.

The psychological part of this kind of losing happens in its own dimension. Names, say, or recollections from the past, can be temporarily forgotten or crowded out of view, yet remain somewhere on the premises. Don't we all experience it from time to time—those of us who are older, especially: the delayed reaction recovery? I will search for a person's name; I'll try every memory prompt I can think of, and when it still won't come, I know to step back. I trust the inner recovery process, which mostly works, but, alas, is seldom on cue. The party ended hours ago, but there I am, back home: "Jennifer—of course! Jennifer . . ."

All of this losing and finding includes the unconscious associations that bring me what I didn't know I was looking for but, as it turns out, needed after all. I'm especially interested in these phenomena as they pertain to writing. In my view, writing, at least literary writing, is not just a matter of inventing out of whole cloth or drawing on what we remember, but also of accessing sought-for words and connections. Do we, when we're writing, *reach in* to actively find the parts of our next sentence, or are those "given" to us? It often feels like the latter, which naturally makes me wonder: through what agency? Where there is a gift, it is said, there must be a giver.

~

Hoping to better understand the creative act, I look to a metaphor drawn from Stendhal's book *On Love*. He describes a branch thrown into a flooded salt mine and pulled up months later, encrusted. Salt crystals, he says, work like the accumulation of imaginings and fantasies that create what we think of as love's mystery.

Crystallization might also serve as a metaphor for how our recollections and associations connect with the act of writing, how it is that when you are in that particular, receptive state, words and ideas can seem to auto-generate.

When I'm immersed ongoingly in a project, all sorts of quotes and phrases will come to me unbidden—as often as not while I'm paying attention to something else. Last week, after I'd started this essay, I was driving to New York for the weekend, listening to music and daydreaming, and suddenly I remembered—for no apparent reason—Malcolm Lowry's line: "The lighthouse invites the storm." This is as plain a sentence as Lowry ever put to paper. Why would it suddenly announce itself? Our preoccupations are indeed like branches lowered into the unconscious.

~

In jazz, improvisation is the art of responsiveness, a simultaneous engagement both with the music and with the improvisatory moves of the other musicians. It requires a high attunement as well as an unthinking confidence that it will all come outright. Improvisation requires a creative willingness; it presupposes that the "stuff" is all there, that it only needs to be tapped. One of my favorite quotes early on—I kept it pinned up over my desk for years—was René Crevel's "No daring is fatal." I tried to make myself believe it was true. I wasn't thinking about overt acts of daring, for some are, in fact, fatal. I took it as a necessary wisdom about creativity.

The quotation triggers another memory. Long before coming to Boston, I lived for some seasons in Biddeford Pool, an oceanside town in southern Maine. I walked the beach and the shoreline daily. There was a vast jumble of rocks and tidal pools, and at low tide it presented a fabulous obstacle course. It was not long before I had devised a ritual. I would start at one end—barefoot—and walk as fast as I could across the expanse. Barnacles, clear spots, rough edges. I was not allowed to *think* a path, I had to trust my feet to find the right way and avoid getting gashes. And so long as I didn't think while I made my way across—teetering, exhilarated—I was fine.

This was a time when I was also enamored of the idea of bricolage. As I remember, I found the word in Lévi-Strauss, maybe his *Tristes Tropiques*. Bricolage was, as I understood it, the art of making do with whatever was at hand. Life-improvisation.

~

The French seem to own this style of openness, or at least some of its characteristic words. Along with *bricolage*, derived from the French word *bricoler*, which means "to putter about," there is the concept of the flâneur. As featured by Baudelaire and, later, Walter Benjamin, the flâneur is an idler, a wanderer who has no destination and is therefore open to everything equally. He (or his counterpart, the flâneuse) is the emblem of a desirable freedom and also of an expanded way of looking. When we have a destination—as we usually do—we are occupied with getting there, and our vision necessarily narrows.

The flâneur, meanwhile, is chance incarnate. While he is not really "lost"—for he has no destination—he represents the possibility of finding. He can direct his attention wherever he chooses, and there is no predicting what surprises he will come upon. But what about the other, less literal landscape: the landscape of time. Are there ways to wander there as well? What else is Proust's epic *In Search of Lost Time?* And what of Walter Benjamin? He conducts a kind of literary flânerie in his long essay "Berlin Childhood," in which he brings the two realms together, laying out memories of his childhood in terms of specific locales, heeding no particular chronology, obeying the idiosyncratic principle of his own remembering.

~

On one of my days in New York, I decided I would walk the High Line, the elevated urban trail that runs from Thirty-fourth Street to Twelfth. It was crowded, and I found that the best way to proceed was by sauntering. Slowing down was a pleasure. The leisurely pace allowed me to look around more carefully—the brickwork of old buildings, massive steel projections, and lots of crazily reflecting glass. It was not long before I had my phone out and was snapping at a high rate. This was one of those times when everything seemed a likely subject.

It was no surprise that Walter Benjamin once again intruded on me. In his essay "The Work of Art in an Age of Mechanical Reproduction," he writes: "Every day the urge grows stronger to get hold of an object at very close range by way of its likeness." If the urge was strong back then, I thought, it has now become a collective obsession. Not only was I succumbing, but so was everyone else. I looked around and saw, as in a dream, crowds of people doing just what I was doing. Harvesting images—or was it plundering? Whether taking selfies against the skyline, collecting evidence of a trip or experience, or like me, hoping to capture an artistic image, we were, as Benjamin would have it, collectively stripping the essential otherness from our physical surroundings. It was hard not to wonder how Benjamin's sustained visual "taking" might be changing the way we perceive and experience the world.

Don DeLillo's *White Noise* deals with this question. I'm thinking in particular of the chapter in which self-styled culture theorist Murray Siskind goes off on a riff about a barn that he and his friend are visiting. The structure has been advertised as "the most photographed barn in America." People come from far and wide with their cameras, and Murray watches them go to work. "Being here is a kind of spiritual surrender," he observes. "We see only what the others see. The thousands who were here in the past, those who will come in the future. We've agreed to be part of a collective perception. It literally colors our vision."

Murray is fascinated by the tautology of something being famous for being famous, and how people's picture-taking is in fact a participation in a collective supposition. He concludes that "[O]nce you've seen the signs about the barn, it becomes impossible to see the barn." Take enough photographs of anything and reality is leached away.

Once I subscribed completely to Murray's view. But my thinking began to change when I started taking photos with my phone and experimenting with possibilities. True, I may be sapping reality in my small way, but I have also become much more attentive to my surroundings. I now look at the world around me opportunistically, assessing the image-value of each thing. Details are more vivid as I single them out. I am less absorbed in the immediacy of participation—a real loss—but the counterpoint gain has been an excitement about looking that I haven't felt since the world was young—grant me that slight exaggeration. Going through my days, I pause again and again. I find myself framing what's in front of me—framing and magnifying. This is not a conscious process, though at first it might have been. It is now part of how I encounter the world—with or without my phone.

~

The idea of a conscious versus unconscious process also applies to taking photographs. There is the matter of peripherality, for one thing—the attending that happens when the mind is focused elsewhere. Most pictures I take now are corner-of-the-eye. Something in my field of vision "catches my eye" and I stop. I have come to trust this reflex. My unconscious, I've realized, is a far better photographer than my determined and seeking self. More and more I heed the signals from my deeper self—if it is in fact deeper and not just other.

There was a book I went back to often in college when I was nurturing my dreams of becoming a writer. It was a compendium called *The Creative Process*, and it was packed with personal accounts by writers, artists, and scientists of their "aha!" moments. The one I remember best was by the German chemist August Kekulé. He had been working for years to determine the structure of benzene and had reached a point of intense frustration. The story, very Jungian, I think, is that he dozed off one night and dreamed of snakes coiling to reach their own tails. When he woke, he had it—what became known in chemistry as the "benzene ring."

I don't feel quite the same frustration with writing, and I don't think I have dreams related to projects I am working on. However, I do wake up and find, very often, that ideas and structural insights have germinated in the night. I've been given some new angle on the day's task. Something previously hidden has moved into range—that's the feeling anyway. I can lie in bed and muse productively on the next step.

~

I've always been fascinated by constraint, how it is at once a curb and a liberation. I used to talk about this with writing students who protested that they had nothing to say. I assured them that if I were to lock them in a room with a single initiating prompt, they would, after a time, be astonished by what they could pull out of themselves. They would find a way to tap the part of the mind that works by association. The branch thrown into the mine.

The dynamics of prodding are elusive. How is it that we can't tickle ourselves, but if poked under the arm by someone else's finger we go into a paroxysm? It's the same with writing. I can be utterly at a loss for a long spell, but if I'm then asked to write on a specific subject, almost right away my brain switches modes. Ideas rush like metal filings to the proverbial magnet. The lighthouse, the storm. No less interesting—to continue the trope—is how, as I read back through, these ideas feel true to my own patterns of thinking.

~

The opposite of *constrained* might well be *aleatory*, by which I mean shaped by chance. *Aleatory* has its root in *alea*, the Latin word for *dice*, and is conceptually close kin to the improvisatory. But there is an important difference. The aleatory lets the chips, dice, or yarrow stalks fall where they may, thus revealing a singular cross-section of the moment. Improvisation, by contrast, emphasizes surprise connections and in its way moves to create artistic meaning.

Merriam-Webster has this to say:

"*Aleatory* was first used in English in the late 17th century to describe things that are dependent on uncertain odds, much like a roll of the dice. The term now describes things that occur by sheer chance or accident. . . . Going a bit further, the term *aleatory music*, or *chance music*, describes a musical composition in which certain parts are left for the performer to concoct through improvisation."

That "sheer chance" is pretty unambiguous, but the last point— that chance music *describes a musical composition in which certain parts are left for the performer to concoct through improvisation*—brings the two together: chance and intent. The performer adapts and transforms unforeseen givens. In this way, improvisation opens a window on the unconscious interactions of memory and association, without which there could be no art.

(2019)

Ten Broad Swipes
at the Problem of Structure

One: There is, of course, the specter of arbitrariness. For I could just as well have proposed five or fifteen such swipes. Obviously I am using the idea of a list as an opening gambit, a triggering prompt, and in fact I don't know how many understandings I have about structure—though my presumption is that I have some, or else the idea of writing about structure would not likely have occurred to me.

The first thing I would offer—philosophically—is that at a certain not-even abstract level the structure embodies the necessity of the expression, what might be called the writer's relation to the subject. The structure diagrams his or her psychological organization of that subject, and as such it is itself expressive. I mean, it not only *conveys* content, but in its way of conveying is itself a kind of content. I'm not trying to be whimsically tautological here. As we all know, there is a huge difference between a narration that unfolds an experience in sequence (as they say in the movies, when the witness is being questioned, "Just start at the beginning…") and one that invents its own logistics, jumping to and fro, weaving hindsight perspectives in with accounts of original impressions, or else making a delicate or indelicate braid, alternating points of view and time-sequences in some strategically managed way.

What, then, I wondered, might be the effect of subjecting this great and vastly mutable issue of expressive structure to a format which is essentially arbitrary, proposing an accumulation of observations and insights with no inherent priority or culmination—using numbers not as a ranking of importance, but merely as a neutral way of saying: Here are ten things you might think about. I had always considered the numbered essay a faux form, but here was a chance to get some use out of it.

Two: This notion of numeration brings us directly up against the idea of constraint. For isn't it true that every form, every laying-out of contents, is also of necessity obedient to an idea of limit? To determine to write an essay or a book—or a series of books—is to propose to oneself a preliminary confining shape. I settled on the number ten quite arbitrarily—not, as I noted, because I knew that I had ten things to say, but rather because I thought, "If I have ten units to work with, if I challenge myself with that specificity, I will, one way or another, have put a corral around the subject." I have a sense about how my mind works, and I know that the number, the expectation of format, will exert influence on my thinking as I proceed.

But then, don't we all do this? Isn't most of what we do as writers a kind of engagement, or a to-fro exchange, with the grand arbitrariness of our unstructured internal life? I decide to adopt *ten* as my guideline, and then use it as a lever on my thinking process. If I find, as may happen, that I have many more than ten things to say, I will be forced to prioritize, consolidate, and edit. If, as is much more likely, I discover that I have many *fewer*—then I will have to look for ways to grow what I have. I will push harder at certain points, create subdivisions where I might otherwise not have done so . . . Understand that I'm using this idea of making a numbered list mainly as an example, a way of getting at the kind of thing we do with any conceptual premise that we adopt.

I remember something that the poet Joseph Brodsky said in an
interview once: "The thing is," he said, "that you can always go on,
even when you have the most terrific ending. For the poet, the credo
or doctrine is not the point of arrival but is, on the contrary, the point
of departure for the metaphysical journey. For instance, you write a
poem about the crucifixion. You have decided to go ten stanzas—and
yet it's the third stanza and you've already dealt with the crucifixion.
You have to go beyond that and add something—to develop it into
something which is not there yet. Basically what I'm saying is that the
poetic notion of infinity is far greater, and it's almost self-propelled
by the form."

"Self-propelled by the form." The suggestion is that the form,
the structure, is itself a kind of intelligence; it helps lead forth the
content—*educes* it—and the written piece is its education.

Three: A constraint is a fixed prohibition, a boundary against which
something—expression—*strains*. For a writer, it is all-important.
Because no matter what one's subject, it is—in theory—inexhaustible. We think of Tennyson's "Flower in a Crannied Wall," of which
he wrote: "Flower in the crannied wall, / I pluck you out of the crannies, / I hold you here, root and all, in my hand, / Little flower—but
if I could understand / What you are, root and all, and all in all, / I
should know what God and man is."

Given world enough, and time, all things can be seen to connect.
To talk or write about anything you have to put up exclusionary boundaries everywhere, or risk chaotic proliferation. Therefore you need a
way in, the right way. And if there is not one absolute approach—how
could there be?—there are more and less viable ones. Just as possibili-

ties need to be encouraged and generated, they also need to be steadily reined in, policed. And here the constraint is a friend, a desirable thing. As writers, we learn to adapt constraints to our needs. There are, naturally, many kinds. The ones that interest me here are those that are useful in the discovery of our inner materials—contents—as much as in the subsequent shaping of those materials. If someone says to me, for instance, "Write a ten-page essay on the idea of virtue," that is a constraint. The instruction gives me the scope and scale of my thinking, though it tells me nothing to help determine what that thinking will be. Still, even that basic assignment offers me a first basis for trawling and then sifting what I may know or think without necessarily being aware of knowing or thinking. And if that someone were then to specify, "Write ten pages on virtue in the Internet age," I would be halfway launched. The specificity creates a narrowing filter of inquiry; it guides me toward what I know.

But no, it does more than guide. This is something I've learned from years of writing: it also activates a kind of magnet. Which is to say, it provokes to life an inner process whereby ideas of a certain kind are more apt to occur. And in this way it offers the heartening confirmation of something we often forget: which is that we possess far more in the way of ideas and insights than we know, and that they are lying in wait, pending articulate expression. Isn't this a version of what we discover reading Plato, the *Dialogues*, wherein over and over we see the teacher Socrates lead his chosen interlocutor, by way of questions, into making more refined assertions, into—why not say it?—*thinking*. Socrates turns whomever he interrogates into a philosopher, revealing to them that they have all along possessed great untapped reserves of insight.

Constraint is the tension against which the undisciplined "stuff" of consciousness tests itself. Released impulses do not merely float free—they are shaped by certain expectations. The injection of the tension of constraint provokes certain psychic elements out of dormancy, roiling them, rendering them active, but also subjecting them to the first tentative formulations of order.

Four: Speaking of order, the *idea* of order—and illustrating the associative process that is one kind of generative mental activity—I think of Wallace Stevens' wonderful poem "Anecdote of the Jar," which seems to me exactly to the point:

> I placed a jar in Tennessee,
> And round it was, upon a hill.
> It made the slovenly wilderness
> Surround that hill.
>
> The wilderness rose up to it,
> And sprawled around, no longer wild.
> The jar was round upon the ground
> And tall and of a port in air.
>
> It took dominion everywhere.
> The jar was gray and bare.
> It did not give of bird or bush,
> Like nothing else in Tennessee.

What is this little poem but a parable of writing? To appropriate, and then radically simplify, its conceit: the wilderness can be seen as the vast chaos of the unconscious, and the jar as the thought, the idea, the constraint around which all the chaos organizes itself. Because, as I have been suggesting, chaos aspires to form; disorder fulfills itself in order—at least where there is the presence of purposeful consciousness. Very Germanic, this. Nietzsche, Mann . . . It could also be the most heartening, possibly exciting, thing about our human sentience, its coherent generativity. I'm back to proposing assignments, prompts. Let's say I insist that you write for an hour about asparagus. You have no choice, you are my prisoner. Your first thought might well be: But I have nothing to say about asparagus. Second thought: Except, well, maybe . . . And then at some point, I almost guarantee it: *Voila!* As in: *I had no idea I had so much to say about asparagus.*

Five: So far I have been mainly talking about constraint, using it to mine the self, and not yet about my ostensible topic, structure. Though, of course, structure is itself a constraint. But it is also, in another sense, its opposite. For, unlike constraint—and apart from what I am doing here with my arbitrary numeration—structure in the way I'm conceiving it, as part of the creative process, is not imposed from without. No, it evolves from within, obeying the needs of the expression. It is, as I said, the shape of the writer's psychological engagement with the subject. Structure, maybe even more than the specific ideas or contents of any work, is what confers the idea of necessity. The shape, the proportion, and the organization, relation of part to part, signal to the writer (and eventually to the reader) whether this is an organically viable expression or not.

The big and vexatious question for the writer is: how do we find structure? But also: *is* it something we find, or—to make the glib-seeming but relevant reversal—does it find us? How much do we actively control the workings of our creative process? To try to answer this we should consider more closely what structure *is* in an essay, and what it is not.

It is not, almost ever, a simple chronological account of something that happened, or a logically straightforward laying-out of a theme or an idea. Certainly not in any essay that makes use of the first-person pronoun. Even as narratively forthright a piece as George Orwell's classic "Shooting an Elephant"—which *does* proceed mainly as a sequence of events—is embedded in the larger frame of subjective time, so that the author begins with an anticipatory set-up and concludes by stepping away to assess the impact that his experience had on him years later.

The essay takes its power from Orwell's way of situating his account in the past and then compressing the hindsight interval so that he can spring his belated recognition on the reader with maximum effect. Use of the first person inevitably introduces time as dimensionality, creating what feels like the correlative of spatial depth. Or else I think of Joan Didion's classic "Goodbye to All That," which would appear to follow the basic trajectory of her years living in New York, but which in fact evokes such a spatialized and associative sense of subjective interiority that notions of sequence are rendered essentially moot.

The subject of the personal essay or memoir is almost never just *what happened.* To find her way in, the writer needs to identify the whole psychological experience, which is to say not just the event, but the responses to the event over time which constitute its realized meaning—all that which makes the writing worthwhile or necessary. And then: how to bring the reader into that experience? Which part *was* the real experience? The event, or the recognition of its importance over time?

There is no universal rule for creating structure, no one-size-fits-all principle that will avail, though our schooling in five-paragraph themes has given us a lot to undo—mainly the assumption that there is an accepted way. But ultimately there is only the unique way—the unrepeatable dramatization of the author's engagement with her subject—which is to say, so often, her engagement with herself over time.

Six: The *what* and the *how*. So much about structure comes down to this: identifying what it is that agitates and excites the writer-mind, which of course is not the same as the regular mind, making some determination of the scale and extent of the material, and then deciding how to pitch it, finding the necessary tone. *Tone* is, in essence, establishing the self's relation to the material. It is not a minor component of the process, some last-minute nicety, but every bit as critical as timing is for the comic. Without the right tone the writer is lost to his subject, it to him. What we glibly call writer's block is often an inability to locate the right tonal (and rhythmic) address. I can't say how many times I've fretted myself into a knot trying to write an essay one way, concluded impossibility—only to have a sentence emerge in some completely different register, whereupon I suddenly see it all, and it feels like all I can do to keep up with the material. And by this I mean not just the words, but also the sequence, the structural transitions that can feel like they are being telegraphed from some control center. Indeed—and this is so telling—very often with the discovery of the right, natural-seeming tone comes the recognition of the right place for the piece to begin. As if the logic of the whole comes wrapped inside the sound, the cadence. For me it is seldom vice-versa.

Seven: Here is a short domestic parable. I'm in a state. I'm hunting all through the house for something I need, and though I can't find it anywhere, I'm also almost seeing it in each place I look. As if it can not *not* be there. The certainty keeps me going. The art of losing may not be hard to master, but making peace with the idea of loss is. To not be able to find something you know has to be right here. Has to be because I put it in a place so that it could be found when needed. Which means that looking for it is really more like looking for myself as I was—a version of getting inside the mind of the criminal to solve the crime. If you know the motive and the psychology . . .

Some version of this "where is it?" attends the writing process—always, though it's also different. The part of what we put to the page that we don't fully know is the *why* of doing it. We trust that the act of expression will deliver it and free us from the restless chafe of at least this one incompletion. "I know it's here somewhere, I can almost see it." And with this feeling, this agitated intuition, we are back to the idea of the unconscious.

In a recent writing workshop there was a general conversation about what does and doesn't belong in an essay—how we determine the scale and extent of the subject in question. One student described how she'd been scrambling to note down everything she thought might be useful, which is to say noting down a great deal—for who ever knows what might be just the needed thing? To this I proposed my counter-theory, that there exist important levels of forgetfulness, and that writers might want to learn to use them. These psychic lacunae are different for everyone, of course. Myself, I very deliberately do *not* write down the fleeting images and phrases that come to me while I'm driving, grinding coffee beans, pedaling on my exercise bike. Some of this is owing to laziness, true, but there is also an underlying aesthetic conviction, and Kafka said something of the sort in one of his diaries, that if something is at all worthy, the psyche will retain it; and that, with trust, that thing will resurface when most needed. *With trust.* Take a pause for the emphasis to sink in. In fact, I would go even further and assert that this is the way such important elements ought to come—as *re*surfacings, and not as notations retrieved from a notebook and inserted just because the conscious writing mind decides that they belong there.

The truths we seek as writers often live at a depth, preserving themselves from the erosions of banal dailiness; for that reason they do not yield themselves up easily. Nor can they be gotten at by straightforward means. As often as not, they have to be tricked forth by the solicitations of rhythm or quasipoetic idea-association. As the poet

Tomas Tranströmer wrote: "Beauty you can only see hastily from the side"—which is to say: inadvertently, in ambush. When our truths do come, however, they often carry a crackle of surprise—but also, if this is not a contradiction, a distinct meshing sense of rightness.

Eight: What does this have to do with remembering and forgetting and the unconscious? For me, the whole business goes back to the ancient Greek concept of *anamnesis*, the gist of which is that all knowing is a remembering—that we have no basis for understanding anything that we do not already in some way know. This is a highly compressed way of saying, as certain philosophers did, Plato of course among them, that we are born with the basic structure of knowledge inside us and that our learning is a process of recovering this implanted knowledge. *In the order in which we need it.* For truth, like most things, resonates most fully in context, what Auden called "the valley of its saying." And the recovery of these contexts is the true biography of our higher consciousness.

Nine: First and last things. It is time to look at the question of tone and the enormous philosophical implications of the first sentence. The right first sentence: that from which everything flows. It is not, therefore, just a sentence, but a kind of foreseeing of the whole piece—setting out in its first words the tonal flavor, the attitude, the angle of regard, and immediately suggesting what will and will not be possible for the essay that follows. The first sentence locates the attitude, which is there in the tone and cadence; it also—often—declares the departure in space and time, and gives the first indication of the logic of unfolding—whether it will be retrospective, action-centered, or reflective.

First sentences are fascinating to contemplate because of the contrast between the ostensible finite specificity of the topic and the enormity of implication. It's a paradoxical kind of self-reflexiveness: to get the right first sentence, you need to understand the essay; to realize the essay you need the right first sentence. It captures the pulse. It's like counting off in jazz; establishing the first string of notes. Retrospectively, of course, the first sentence of every good essay (or story, or novel) seems inevitable. To get to the essay, the writer has to find the inevitability of the first sentence. The whole business feels almost mystical—for doesn't it seem that one is not so much inventing it as *discovering* it?

How does this work? You may not first discover the words themselves, but I think you *do* come upon the tone and cadence—and with that, as part of it, as a kind of confirmation, the words often arrive. But again, what determines the tone? What *is* tone? It is, among other things, the specific pressure that feeling and sensibility exert on expression. It is attitude, psychological point-of-view. The question is, can you find the right tone if you have not matured in relation to your subject? Or if it, rather, has not matured in you? Shakespeare wrote that "ripeness is all," and here is one instance of what he meant. You have the tone when what you want to say has ripened within you.

This may seem to contradict my earlier observations about using constraint as a spur, a galvanizing agent. For how could any writer find apt expressive tone for a subject not ripened from within but imposed from without? I nod to the contradiction. And I can only suggest that the pressure of the improvisational—the ad hoc—situation can allow an end-run around a writer's usual ways of moving in on a subject, can channel the surprise of unexpected connections. This can jump-start—or ambush—tone.

Ten: Our revels are now ended, or will be soon, not because the topic has been fully dealt with—how could it be?—but by my own fiat.

By the imposition of the constraint of closure. The fact of having reached, or achieved, number ten, changes everything. Where with earlier numerals there was a somewhat arbitrary feeling of accumulation, now there is a definite imperative of closure. Some ideas have been ventured, and what is wanted are the reflections that would retroactively confer an impression of purpose, of *intendedness*. So that never mind the deliberately form-disrupting nature of this particular form, there is nonetheless a sense that it was done for a reason, achieved by some perverse anti-strategy as its aim: to say things that are important and necessary in a way that gratifies. A very tall order, that. But at the same time it's true that closure is a force that can produce powerful effects. I wrote of openings, and how, ideally, the first sentence will not only establish the tone and cadence—the attitude—of the piece to come, but that it will also, through its vantage, its location in time, establish something of the necessity of the structure.

Endings are no less important. Though it is not for endings to create the voice or propose the logic of the work. Rather, it is for them to signal that the subject has been dealt with. Endings convey, in their substance as well as their tones, the sense of arrival. However an essay begins, the vibration of its last sentence is what the reader carries away. That vibration ought to feel of a piece with all that preceded it, and at the same time be a gathering up of assertions and implications. All writers writing endings trade on cessation—on the effect that silence has on what immediately came before. Which is, almost as a rule, that of an exponential underscoring. Any sentence chased by lasting silence augments itself; it curves around in the reader's mind, attracts meanings and valences it might otherwise not have possessed. How does this work? In part, I think, it is a retroactive effect: as soon as the ending is clearly at hand, the reader or listener reconfigures what preceded it as part of a culmination. There is also the intuiting, affecting us subliminally, of all that might yet be said but is not: the thrust of excised possibility. Not to mention the universally understood archetype: our journey here is over. In having taken us, and now in having stopped, it resembles all other journeys—including the one we are still in the midst of.

But I digress . . . Endings, like beginnings, are the key element of structure. A beginning telegraphs that, however prolific with possibilities, a thing may be undertaken. And in just this way the ending communicates, through the simple fact of cessation, that that thing can also be set aside, laid to rest. It has finitude; it is but a partial transcription of experience. Between beginning and ending—numbers two through nine, if you will—the thing itself, that expression whose architecture is sketched out in the opening words, whose ending is already latent there.

As it was here as soon as I wrote my own opening words, "There is, of course, the specter of arbitrariness." It is a specter that I hoped to challenge and partly subdue. I assumed I would as soon as I wrote those words. For writing is nothing if not a constant defiance of just that. It is a line-by-line manufacture of order, its imperatives so strong that even a purely arbitrary numerical premise will be seen to pull toward a larger coherence. Writing is a steady negotiation between unconscious impulses and rational imperatives, wilderness and jar, and then, of course, the silence that deepens and extends after the last word has been written.

(2014)

Caress the Detail—Thoughts on Repair

They say "God is in the details" or, alternatively, "The Devil is in the details." We've heard it both ways, and have maybe even wondered if God and Devil didn't share something in common. The former phrase is variously attributed to German art historian Aby Warburg or German-born architect Mies van der Rohe. Detail: *Bildausschnitt*. I've been stuck on the first version for a long time, mulling it as one mulls a koan—never quite breaking through but feeling mildly enlightened from the effort expended. Detail is much on my mind these days, whether as a reader, writer, picture-taker, or teacher of writing. I've become more and more aware of its central place in art, not to mention everything else. So much depends on it. And yes, your reflexive association is not misplaced. Those last words light the neural path to William Carlos Williams' over-quoted poem about the wheelbarrow, a poem which right now has its uses:

The Red Wheelbarrow

so much depends
upon

a red wheel
barrow

> glazed with rain
> water
>
> beside the white
> chickens

I didn't at first intend to go here, but that automatic association actually offers me a good lead-in to my subject. Rendered almost invisible through repetition and endless cute parodies by fellow poets—after all, so much can depend on almost anything—the poem enacts an ironic paradox. For while it is itself in large part about the importance of attention, proposing real seeing as a way of countering the contempt-inducing onslaught of the familiar—*slow down and look!*—its status as "a poem everyone knows" has made it almost impervious to attention.

Williams uses his famously effective line breaks to stagger the eye's movement down the page, so that we perform at least three psycho-optical operations while reading. First, we see the somewhat generic "red wheelbarrow"; second, we zoom in on the glaze of rainwater, so that even if we did not picture the wheelbarrow at first, now we are almost forced to. Then, third, lest we stay confined to the flat plane of that depiction, Williams introduces the adjacent white chicken, and with that one detail we go three dimensional. We almost can't not call up a barnyard scene. On a more basic visual level, there's the satisfying juxtaposition of bright red and white, of inanimate and animate. Not bad for a mere sixteen words.

~

Not long ago, I went to the Boston Museum of Fine Arts. I intended to see a photo exhibition, but it was not yet open to the public, so I ended up taking a long-overdue tour of the various collections. As in most museums, pride of place was given to the big—I guess you could say "white male"—canvases of the eighteenth and nineteenth centuries, which overwhelm the viewer with depictions of disasters at sea, or especially vivid scenes from the Bible or mythology. I moved past them quickly, not really heeding, no longer *seeing*, just as one tends not to see that red wheelbarrow anymore.

But then, traversing a well-lit hallway linking two exhibition spaces, I was stopped mid-stride by something quiet and radiant on the right wall. It was the first small canvas in what appeared to be a row of Dutch still-lifes. The label identified it as "Still Life with Glasses and Tobacco," 1633, by Willem Claesz Heda. I was fixated, pulled in. I let my eyes graze slowly over the densely arranged surface; I followed the visual path leading me from one point to the next. Then, when I'd finally had enough of looking, I found myself asking the obvious question. *Why?* Why did I stop here and not before the voluptuous Renoirs, the grand Delacroix?

I want to pursue this question. But before I do, I need to describe the staged ordinariness of the subject. We are looking at a tabletop strewn with the accoutrements of an evening's pleasure: three olives, a half-filled wine glass, some long clay pipes, a paper holding loose tobacco, a lemon, what looks like a tipped candle holder . . . There is no narrative order. It looks completely haphazard, giving the feel of something just come upon, certainly not a display intended. A quick thumbnail tour of Heda's many other still-lifes, however, reveals that he made painting after painting of this same basic array, sometimes with a bottle, or an oyster, or a fish. Clearly it was not the how-it-was of one fortuitous moment that he was after, but the various atmospheric possibilities of color, of slightly different arrangements of shapes, of light.

Whatever Heda had devised with this particular still-life worked for me. I was completely drawn into that framed-off bit of world. But now I do want to ask, "What was the draw?"

Looking closer, I can separate out various basic elements: the

overall look of the late-day light, the palette of somber hues punc-
tuated by the brightness of the lemon, the glint of light on glass and
candleholder, the shine of the long pipes. Then there is the physical
distribution of the objects, the way the lemon peel, candleholder rim,
and wineglass make a 45-degree angle, and how the horizontal placement of the pipes works to pull the eye full-circle. And of course it is
a separate pleasure just to remark on the fineness of the brushwork.

To look at the painting is to be drawn gradually into a contemplation of its details. The visual complexity—the density—is such
that these details hold the viewer and keep the gaze circulating. The
sustained engagement makes me feel that I have moved into the silence
surrounding these objects; that I have been transferred to another
time frame, one completely counter to the tempo of the lives we live
today. Again, detail.

Detail is the lever of attention. Detail can also be a trigger back
to the fresher vision of childhood—not so much a full-out regres-
sion, more a kind of flash intimation. Our early years were, very likely,
the last time we lived fully in the realm of immediacy and particularity, had not yet gotten caught up in more distracted ways of living
and more abstract modes of thought. I remember how I studied the
world, taking in everything in my available range—the underside of
the dining room table, the odd-looking old tools in the garage drawer,
the way the water made a vortex as it left the tub. My child-world was
a duration world, and I still feel a touch of that when my attention is
deeply engaged.

~

One of the great masters of detail is Nabokov—in most of his work,
but maybe especially in *Speak, Memory*. A detail-glutton by disposition,
he indulges himself in this book with a fierce virtuosity. No detail is
too small or petty for him to evoke. And in the success of the evoca-
tion, he confirms the power that can be found in that smallest thing.

In *Speak, Memory*, he was not merely writing an account of his childhood and coming-of-age. He was bent, like Proust, on repossessing what he'd lost by growing up—what we've all lost. He believed that his feats of observation and recollection could install him back in the sensation-world of *then*.

Looking for a single passage to quote in illustration, I encountered the paralysis I feel studying a good menu. Finally, I decided to open the book at random. What I landed on is a section that recounts Nabokov's experience studying with his "drawing master" as a boy in St. Petersburg:

> *I was captivated by his use of the special eraser he kept in his waistcoat pocket, by the manner in which he held the page taut, and afterwards flicked off, with the back of his fingers, the "gutticles of the percha" (as he said). Silently, sadly, he illustrated for me the marble laws of perspective: long, straight strokes of his elegantly held, incredibly sharp pencil caused the lines of the room he created out of nothing (abstract walls, receding ceiling and floor) to come together in one remote hypothetical point with tantalizing and sterile accuracy.*

The paragraph goes on, but I think the point is made. The detailing underscores the intensity of his childhood awareness, and as we situate ourselves behind the child's eyes, the natural vigilance we still keep resonates, returns us for a moment to the older way of feeling the world. As readers we realize that the language and expression are not a young boy's, but, oddly, this is not a problem. Nabokov's fantastic nuances bring us very close to the child's perceptual world ("by the manner in which he held the page taut, and afterwards flicked off, with the back of his fingers, the 'gutticles of the percha' . . ."). The language belongs to a sophisticated and ironic adult, but the details themselves are ones most plausibly taken in by a child. This moment, packed with quiet surprise, may also render his first real grasp of perspective.

~

Several years ago, the gift of an iPhone activated my dormant lifelong interest in photography, and I joined the growing ranks of ardent amateurs. My incessant snapping has slowly taught me what my eye responds to, and following any number of highly skilled photographers on Instagram has convinced me that one's images, when looked at in series, reveal a pattern almost as distinctive as a prose style. The various visual and compositional decisions come together to make an original amalgam, the elements of which include choice of subject, framing, vantage, and angle, selection of focal distance, use of filters, etc. I can now scroll my Instagram feed and quite often identify the image-taker's name without checking.

Looking at my posts with some detachment, I recognize my own distinguishing commonalities. I have an interest in slightly off-kilter framing, in intense areas of light on objects; a definite preference for the darker side of the palette, and, maybe most tellingly, a way of searching out the point where a known thing shades into abstraction— but never so far that the subject can't be identified. Also, more often than I would have thought, I respond to little anomalies that might suggest a background narrative, if only obliquely.

I have also learned to trust my corner-of-the-eye—which is to say nearly unconscious—responses to the world around me. I often catch myself making what I think of as a photographer's double-take. When something halts me, it's because in some way it cuts against expectation. I think of Roland Barthes' *studium/punctum* distinction, where the former is the expected image, and the latter the often almost-imperceptible detail that changes the perception, suggesting a kind of ghost-narrative. A shadowy forest path may be my ostensible subject, but the glimpse I catch of a child's miniature watch in the grass is an anomaly. If I then decide to take the photo, my impulse is to frame it in such a way that the watch is barely noticeable. The viewer comes upon it only after taking in the tall trees and the cloud parade above them.

In expressive works of all artistic genres, we often see that a detail juts out because the artist or author has subtly—or not—singled it out. We heed the image of Nabokov's drawing teacher holding the paper taut and flicking off bits of eraser *with the back of his fingers*. Such a negligible action. But as we are made to picture that flicking, we draw from it a hint of the teacher's character.

~

When I teach writing students, I become a one-trick pony, making the same basic points about detail over and over. Using various invented examples, I emphasize to them what a difference there is between writing, say, "The woman's red dress" and "The woman's red dress had a small tear in the sleeve." When we read the first, we create, at best, a vague and general red shape; reading the second, we can't help but form an image in our mind's eye. Not that one would want to give every descriptor a detail, of course, but a few, strategically placed, invest the reader more deeply, and almost force a deceleration.

Nabokov wrote, "Caress the detail, the divine detail," and this might be what he meant. Not everyone agrees with his elevation of detail to sacred status. In fact, when I did a search to make sure I had his wording right, I ran across a reference to an essay by one Tony McKibbin entitled "Reckless Triviality," which tries to take down the master. McKibbin's ruling premise is that Nabokov creates beauty for beauty's sake, and his details are often there as adornments rather than in the service of meaning. McKibbin considers them trivial. I disagree. There is a major distinction between a detail and a triviality. In writing, the detail serves an end, and a triviality is a triviality precisely because it does not. Nabokov deploys every word, every image, with studied aesthetic intent.

I have to come back to the idea of God being in the details. It's the ultimate paradox—more of a brain-bender than the Bible's "And the last shall be first," or Eliot's "In my end is my beginning." Logically it proposes fitting infinity into the tiniest of spaces. Of course we know that it—like those other propositions—is being used metaphorically. But a very great expressive power *can* reside in a detail. Not just any detail—I don't think Warburg or van der Rohe would have meant that—but a key detail situated in the right context. The glaze on the wheelbarrow, the glint of light on the painted goblet, the rubbery crumbs brushed away with the backs of the master's fingers.

Such detail, used in expressive arts, has the power, if only momentarily, to break the fourth wall—the illusionism the work is premised on. It shows how artifice can become the path back to the so-called "real." It also helps explain why so many readers feel that their immersion in a work heightens their sense of reality rather than providing an escape from it. *This* is the real paradox, I think. The more stylized or illusionistic the work, the more shocked we are to encounter the world there. Nabokov's every paragraph is a verbally wrought surface—sophisticated, ironic, playful, and delighting in unusual usages. But when he impales our attention with the point of his pin, pushes us into fully attending to a detail, he seems to break down the wall between the made thing and the reality we live in. Nabokov is not looking to create beauty for its own sake. Beauty here is a hallmark of the thing really seen, and that is a doorway back to the world as it is.

I'm not urging writers, photographers, and painters to lard their work with minutiae. But the judicious detail, as I wrote, is the lever of attention. This seems especially important in our moment, when so many forces are coming together to break such attention as we still possess. Our global political reality comes to us by way of a steady inundation of developments tagged as "breaking news," with each new development immediately dissolved by the next.

Swaddled as we are in this thick wool of distractedness, our focus does not easily come to rest on any one thing. At the same time, our digital living—screen ads, links, not to mention the steady interruptions from our mobile devices, which we can't help but check incessantly— divides and subdivides what remains of that focus.

The need to recover attention is vital for coherence in our private lives and in the public sphere as well. It may seem such a small thing, this capture of attention in a poem or story, but as Archimedes asserted in another context several millennia ago: "Give me a place to stand and I'll move the world." Though our arts may not often directly bear on our complex big-picture reality, they do affect perception—and therefore thought—on every level. In our miasma of distractedness and diffusion, well-placed details can still engage the attention. They point us back to the "other" reality, and may help to revive the recognitions and reflexes we are at such risk of losing.

(2018)

Booze Snow Cone
with Crème De Menthe

I've been thinking about writers' houses, the idea of them, prompted, I suppose, by Brock Clarke's dark satire *An Arsonist's Guide to Writers' Homes in New England*, and A. N. Devers' website Writers' Houses, but really nudged along by more long-simmering preoccupations—about loss and permanence, work and its commemoration, the inward life and its outward evidence. The death of the writer Barry Hannah in 2010 brought all this to the surface, though truth be told it didn't have far to travel. These are, adapting Tim O'Brien's title about soldiers to new uses, the things we carry as writers. We make our words in the here and now, but we aim them at the indeterminate then.

Writers' houses, those officially enshrined dwellings of noted figures, signify on so many levels. They carry symbolic community value, serving as a way for a place to honor itself by honoring one of its own. They have obvious historical archival significance. They are also belt notches for seasoned tourists, and pilgrimage destinations for those who have been affected by the author's work, and seek both to pay homage and, at least in private fantasy, to make contact with the single most elusive essence in the world: creative inspiration.

Though I have been to several of these houses in my life, I am not in any sense a pilgrim. I do not seek them out. If one puts itself directly in my path, and if the writer has meant something to me, I will give in to curiosity. I have been to Ernest Hemingway's house in Key West, William Faulkner's in Oxford, Mississippi, and Ralph Waldo Emerson's right here in Concord. I can't remember any others.

The complexity of these encounters—the saturation of "information," the psychological pollen-count—is almost overwhelming. Most of it is self-generated, taking the form of projections and imaginings. There's only so much we can distill from the material evidence itself—furniture, carpeting, windows and curtains, the inevitable paraphernalia—though there is a certain "scene of the crime" aspect to the whole business. I think of Poe's Dupin casing the premises in "The Purloined Letter," grasping finally that a thing is best hidden in plain sight. But in the rooms of celebrated writers, the crime would be expression, the creation of beauty. And where do we start to look?

Unless there is a docent guide (too often there is), the business unfolds in a peculiar, rich silence. There is an expectation of communion. The visitor walks, alone or on tour, from room to room, taking in the larger mise-en-scène—surveying the domestic environment, creating the inevitable mental pictures: he sat here and this is where he took his meals . . . fascinating on a number of levels, but really this part of the tour is a prelude, a kind of tuning-up. For having walked through the house, admired the pictures and bibelots on the mantel, stared down at the empty bed (always somehow emptier than normally empty beds), we come last to the writer's study, and something changes.

It's not unlike the moment on a shipboard tour when the guide throws open the door to the engine room. Only now it is not a roar we hear, but silence—silence that, like the bed seeming emptier, feels more silent. How do we explain this? How can a negation be further negated? Standing at the place of work, we become aware of layers and kinds of silence, and these can be sifted. First, there is the natural silence of the room, the fact that nothing's really happening here: a few people have gathered to stare at a desk. Now amplify this nothing with the sense of hush that you get when people are being self-consciously and deliberately silent, either thinking reverent thoughts or wanting to look like they are. Then there is the imponderable silence that history contributes—our knowing that whatever happened here happened long ago, that decades empty of sound have been laid down one on top of the other. Finally, most elusive of all, we meet the silence born of listening into: we are not merely heeding the absence of sound, but are heeding it as if it held some surviving trace—the breath of the person working, the scratch of a pen.

It's a complicated transaction that goes on in these places, during these moments of reverie. Don't we all, in listening, hope to get closer to the idea of creation? But it's maddeningly difficult. With another art—painting, say—I can picture the hands in motion, summon the paints and brushes spread out on the tabletop. But trying to call up Emerson writing "Self-Reliance," I am reduced to the most tired of film clichés—the pen in the inkwell, the erratic scrinch of the nib, the blot (!), the wadding-up of the dead-end thought . . . The real business cannot be transmitted; it remains masked by near-inertness—the chin resting on the palm of one hand, the fingers of the other drumming on the desktop while the writer waits for the next words or phrases to decide themselves . . .

Still, we visitors linger, tuning in as best we can, combing the mind's fine mesh through the room as if stray molecules of some original inspiration might yet be captured. There is a permanently naive part of the self that hopes to crack the code, find a way into the mystery of mysteries: how the person sitting in that very chair once found his way to the words that bring such new life to things. But no, try as I might, I meet only my own imaginings projected onto the stage-set in front of me.

~

I got to know Barry Hannah over a period of years. He was a writer-in-residence at the Bennington Writing Seminars where I was teaching, and every summer he visited the campus for four or five days. Modest and self-effacing though he was, his legend insisted on coming along: the wild-boy author of *Airships* and *Ray*, the boozy hellion who once brandished a pistol in a writing workshop to make a point about something (it was never established what) . . . But at this later point in his life Barry played against legend. He drank coffee, smoked cigarette after cigarette, but that was it; the old scene-making was nowhere in evidence—he was low key, polite, and almost Buddhistically attuned to everything around him. But later in the night, when he felt relaxed and started talking, it was clear where the prose came from.

We usually roomed together, with one or two others, in a place called Davis House—alternately "Fort Dix"—and of course there were many late nights of talk. Most often it was not just the two of us. Barry had a serious fan base among students and faculty, and those nights in the kitchen and living room followed the pattern of some uncensored TV sitcom, with people walking on and off, bringing their poisons—Barry always said, "I don't drink anymore, but I like to watch you-all do it." Inevitably, the conversation moved from earnest and focused to a hilarious free-for-all of gossip and storytelling. Barry, of course, was the man with the stories. He had a jazzman's expert timing, a faux-naif's art of insinuation, and, most enjoyable of all, a way of slowly sidling up to the point of whatever he was telling. We were, most of us, his foils, his buttoned-up Northerners.

Over the years Barry and I did get a few quiet times to talk about our families, our work, the writing life in general. Though he affected a Good Ol' Boy's disdain for the preciosity of anything artsy, he was in fact avid for writing talk, forever asking who I was reading, what I was writing about, and what I thought of any number of writers on the scene. Barry also had a keen and competitive fascination with editors, publishers, who was paying what for how many words, and so on.

Once, I remember, I asked him what his home was like, how he set himself up to work, what I would now call the standard *Paris Review* interview kinds of questions. Barry grimaced—he always grimaced before speaking—and laughed his barking laugh and told me that I would be disappointed if I ever saw how he was set up. "It's ordinary, Sven, very ordinary." I assumed he meant that there was nothing at all picturesque or revealing about his house, no hallowed chamber of composition, no great library sanctum. Who could imagine Barry in a sanctum? The idea that any fanfare should attend the artist's— any artist's—doings was abhorrent to him. What I can't remember is whether he said much about what *was* there. Paintings, photographs, motorcycle memorabilia, old guns? I should have listened closer, or asked more, because right now I can't get myself to visualize anything except a generic one-story suburban set-up. That may be all wrong. But whatever he did tell me, he made it clear enough that his was not the kind of place that would pique the avid fan, the literary tourist. I can imagine his voice, Barry mimicking the eyelash-batting enthusiasm of the curator: Oh yes, Mr. Hannah wrote some of his finest work at that very desk, and those black marks all over, those were left by the cigarettes he forgot about when his Muse arrived.

Writers' houses are largely about the myth of inspiration. We see them as the worldly sites where otherworldly activities took place. Yes, I exaggerate. But how much? It's all a matter of degree, the stakes rising with the perceived greatness of the work. I might not get much of a frisson standing in the room where John O'Hara wrote *BUtterfield 8*, but put me at Duino Castle and show me the place where Rilke started the first of his *Elegies* and I might have a different response. It was Rilke, after all, who wrote with such a grand self-celebratory entitlement: "The poet is eternity protruding into time."

~

The other day, in an access of mid-August, mid-life, mid-afternoon boredom, I stretched out on the attic couch and flipped open a book I've been happily nibbling at off and on for months now, Geoff Dyer's *Out of Sheer Rage*. Flipped it, as it happened—I do believe in serendipity sometimes—to a passage where the author goes to visit the D. H. Lawrence museum in the English town of Eastwood. Lawrence was Dyer's hero, his early inspiration, and the whole book is his protracted wrestling with the meaning of Lawrence in his life. Here he writes:

> *Upstairs from the parlor was a bedroom which looked like someone had died in it a century ago or the day before yesterday, whichever was the longer. Off-white, death-colored night-dresses were spread on the bed which looked like it was designed to die in; either for dying in or giving birth in, ideally both at the same time. In a room like this rest seems a species of grief. Museum installations always have a touch of death about them. Houses have to live; they cannot be embalmed. This one died a natural death and then, after it had fallen into disuse, after it had decomposed, they tried to bring it to life again but succeeded only in embalming it in death.*

~

I'm trying to picture myself now—there, in Hannah's ordinary house. I'm sure I've gone too far in the other direction, but I see nothing but ordinary carpeting, ordinary furniture and fixtures, an ambience like what you find in brochures for do-it-yourself remodeling ideas. Ordinary . . . Why has this word been haunting me? Maybe because it is the precise opposite of what Barry was and what he did, and what he is on the printed page so long as there are minds capable of decoding the signs. The man was possessed of an extraordinary sensibility, tragic and exultant and wisely comic in every vein, and he stood outside in Randall Jarrell's thunderstorms (intended for poets) enough times to be struck and struck again by lightning. All of my fussing about houses and desks has been a clumsy effort to get at that edge-of-the-cliff feeling, the sense that right where this world of things—of concrete evidence—runs out, the yonder begins: the place where language transforms the ordinary and the rulebook is put away. Free-flight, unexpectedness renewing itself from sentence to sentence—that's what Barry was about.

There is no greater pleasure, at least in the literary sphere, than picking up a book by a writer you love and finding things to read to others. We look to create a circuit of likemindedness, to pass along what has been given to us. Would Barry have stood for me writing this here? No more than he would have stood for a docent showing his workspace to a group of tourists. But then, he's not here to tell me not to, is he?

On Harold's patient directions, the amused bartender at the Holiday Inn made us a sort of booze snow cone with crème de menthe. I guess I was so healthy and unpolluted, I felt it immediately, my first drink, or suck. I lit up like a pink sponge. All the world seemed at my feet, and I could barely stand the joy of Godot, Natalie Wood, *and Harold in it at the same time. Even the city name, Baton Rouge, was vastly hip. Red stick, red stick. Very way out. Life was a long wonderful thing. It was so good you expected some official to show up and cancel it.* ("Scandal D'Estime")

(2010)

Double Take

> *Whatever the landscape had of meaning*
> *appears to have been abandoned. . . .*
>
> —Elizabeth Bishop

Somewhere in the middle of the journey of my life, after years of determined questioning of our collective technological obsessions, and deploring of one development and another, I found I had myself become enslaved—first by answering machines, then the Internet—thus unhappily confirming the very takeover effect I'd been writing about. I acclimated, as one does, drew new lines in the sand and tried to hold my ground. Last year, however, following my pattern of diminishing resistance and reluctant capitulation, I got a smartphone. There was a logic, of course: I blamed everything on my aging parents. Well past their mid-journey, they had reached a point—the whole family had reached a point—where we had to be able to reach each other whenever we needed. *If it had been up to just me . . .*

So it goes. End of one story, beginning of next story—a story with a surprise in it. For in all my anxious deploring and then defensive rationalizing of this latest choice, I had overlooked one—what would for me become the main—thing. That it was not just a smartphone I had bought. It was also a camera, one so fine and sophisticated and easy to use that in a single leap, via one inadvertent tap of its small camera icon, I got over what had been one of my longstanding frustrations—my inability to incorporate photography into my life. Mea culpa, I'll admit it.

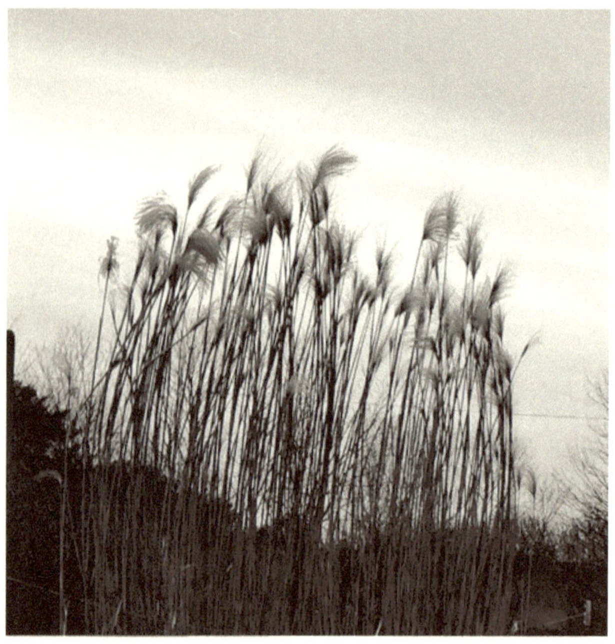

This had everything to do with my lazy unwillingness to learn about shutter speeds, lenses, and darkroom procedures, and my deeply embedded fear of the "technical." Back when I might have gotten started, it seemed that too much equipment was wanted, too much time. How much easier it was to put some words on a page and call myself a writer, to get at reality without all that chemical fuss.

How did this recent quasi-accidental breakthrough come about? I am practiced enough now that a few finger-swipes of my phone screen, of my "camera roll," will take me back to the very moment.

Indeed, I locate my first image, and I see above it the date and time: December 25, 2014. 3:12 p.m. The visual itself—a stand of dried weeds and seedpods—brings the moment back, almost as if I were somehow moving inside that little square and opening it like a tent around me. Yes, it was Christmas Day. I had gone for an afternoon walk in our neighborhood, making my tour of Reed's Brook Park, my regular circuit. Halfway around the pond, prompted by I know not what, I took my new phone from my coat pocket. I think I was curious and had decided to dare an experiment. I remember that I held the phone away from the sunlight and very lightly touched the camera icon in the upper right-hand corner of the screen. A tap. Barely even that.

But it was enough. Because with that tap a fine-grained real-time panorama opened to my eyes. It was exactly what I was standing in front of, only framed in miniature and given an appealing hyper-reality by the heightened camera light. With another experimental touch, this time an act of pinching and widening, I made the camera's view of those dried-out weeds grow into a granular clarity. I very lightly touched the circle marked PHOTO and registered a single pulse-beat of a blink.

Something had just happened, I saw it. And digital tyro though I am, I knew enough to tap the adjacent "photos" icon for a look. I don't know what I was expecting. Certainly not anything so momentous. For, standing there on the path, I registered a genuine lift of excitement. I beheld, upright and sharply textured, bristles cleanly backlit by acetylene blue skies: my weeds. I had come into a new, unforeseen power.

It was not my first "exposure." Photography had been a fascination for me at least since late high school, a time when I got to be friends with a camera obsessive and kept him company in the school darkroom. There I would watch while he clothes-pinned his latest damp black-and-white enlargements to the wires that zigzagged the room. Photos of bums in Detroit's skid row areas—they were the most thrillingly gritty things I'd ever seen. The authentic stuff, no question.

But the real show, for me, was the one that happened when the over-head went off and the red bulb turned on, as my friend unspooled the negatives and worked with the enlarger and the chemical baths. I loved the moments, still so vivid, when the photo paper was first immersed and the darks crept through their various gradations like a magic moss as the chaos of changing tones slowly yielded a clear image.

It took my breath away. A person could never get tired of that ghostly transaction, I thought—and yet, strangely, I did nothing about it. I did not try to do the same, did not sign up for instruction or save my money to buy a camera. Not that I didn't have my fantasies—of course I did. But there were those many obstacles, all that private inertia. The idea of taking pictures remained an idea, a seductive fantasy. I lived it vicariously, which was easy enough to do. This was the late sixties, after all. The hipster photographer with his telephoto lenses and bandolier of film canisters was a cultural icon. I picture the David Hemmings character in Michelangelo Antonioni's 1966 movie *Blow-Up*—the long-haired artiste all revved up and intense, doing his kabuki dance around his near-naked model, contorting to whatever angle he needs to get the desired shot.

The Julio Cortázar story it's based on, so very different from the movie, brought an even greater vibrational gravitas to the act of click-ing a shutter. The synapse-leaping prose, the alchemical implications of the whole process: the transfer of a piece of the world, an image of a piece of the world, to a sheet of chemically treated paper. I was captivated. I incorporated photographs into stories I was writing. A few years later I even tried writing a novel about a photographer—never mind that I knew nothing. All that compulsion, but I would not get myself behind a lens.

Not for decades. Not until that recent—and largely accidental—awakening in Reed's Brook Park, which to most will understandably seem like nothing more than a moment's play. For obviously I'm not pursuing the path of Cartier-Bresson, Weston, Atget, Strand, or any of the others who have used the camera as an instrument of vision. But what are our measures of significance? Something *did* happen there on that path. I stumbled into a new private pleasure—one that has since infiltrated my thinking on many fronts, most immediately my thinking about writing.

~

In the first weeks and months after I discovered what amazing powers were coiled in my new device—the reach of its little lens, its gradations of zoom, the editing operations I could perform on my images—I became everyone's cliché of the smitten amateur. I couldn't help myself. I carried the thing with me at all times. I went out of my way to look for interesting sights and revealing lines of vantage; I stalked subjects. I spent far too much time scrolling through my "archive"—deleting, restoring, but mainly just studying.

It's this "stalking" I want to talk about first, because I see that it corresponds to something very familiar from the writing life. Pondering it now reminds me of how long it took me to learn the difference between thinking my way toward what might be a viable subject, and—very different—letting a subject reveal itself, then trusting the response of my writerly instincts to that revelation.

In that early phase of my new amateurism, I went about in a kind of framing frenzy. I was like one of those caricatured figures always shown squinting at the world through the box made by their thumbs and forefingers. I was constantly assessing whatever was around me for its visual potential, looking to see if it could work as a composition, an arresting image. My idea of what might be suitable—or, better, "interesting"—was mostly the product of enthusiasms, things I'd seen and liked in the work of others. Not surprisingly, I found myself taking close-up shots of vegetables à la Weston, fingers and hands after Stieglitz, or cemetery stones and urns as Atget might have seen them. I don't think I even knew the extent to which the images by these others had shaped how I saw. Nor can I pretend that I'm not still very much in the thrall of just such subjects, or that it's a useless approach.

In fact, though I've started to recognize the extent of my own impulse to mimic, I still venture these deliberated "studies." But I do so now with a kind of literary/essayistic intent. I consider them exercises in attention, and I take my mantra from Flaubert: "Anything becomes interesting if you look at it long enough." The magnifying power of my phone's camera lens started me in this direction. It was obvious and irresistible. But if my initial approach to, say, an impressive Spanish onion was calculated, my findings were often a surprise. I'd had no idea that a highly magnified image of concentric rings could be so visually satisfying, so revealing! Not to have known this was, in part, owing to my own general inattentiveness. But it was also a reminder of the limits of the eye's power. I had not fully recognized the beauty of the onion on the cutting board because I am not capable of that degree of stilled optical focus. After a few such eye-openers, I got greedy with my looking.

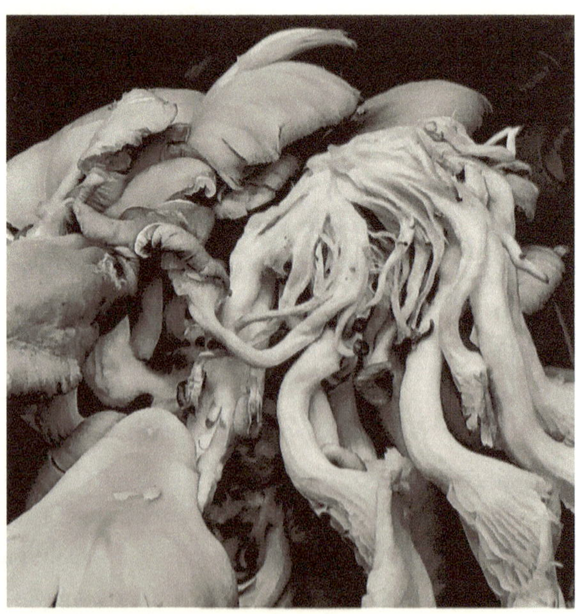

I turned my attention to other things: the stipples on a strawberry, the diaphanous husks of a garlic clove, the bulbous curvature of a clutch of mushrooms. All my life I had taken them in with the most casual of glances. Now I found myself stopping again and again to hover over yet another extraordinary shape.

Though this hyper-immersion in the visual might seem to have no direct bearing on the way I think about writing, it disturbs the category frames—the assumptions—that we all have about the apparent value or importance of one thing over another, undermining and subverting the obeisance we pay to assumed scales of value. It is a small-scale adjustment, a minor subversion, but in fact it has revolutionary potential.

For me, the deep draw of the personal essay has always been that it represents an orchestration of thought, a rendering of how the mind processes experience. This, far more than the pretext—the ostensible occasion of the essay—is the interesting thing. The movement of mind. When I eavesdrop on myself (and this kind of essay writing is nothing if not a form of self-auditing), I often find I am radically skewing what I recognize on another level to be the accepted sequencing and proportioning of things. In that divergence I can feel myself testing my own codes of meaning, looking to see what is true for me.

The actual motions of thought are seldom if ever systematic, and they are often a-logical, obeying mysterious prompts of connection between one thing and another. They map their terrain unexpectedly. Details that some might suppose trivial loom large, and other, supposedly important matters get short shrift. These distinctions—often-unconscious choices we make and how we make them—reveal more clearly than almost anything else the structure of our sensibility. In relation to writing, I had inklings about this for a long time before I could grasp the matter directly. My attraction to various stylists—Cortázar, Woolf, Sebald, Ondaatje—influenced my thinking in important ways, but I credit my reading of Nabokov's *Speak, Memory* as the eye-opening event.

Looking back on his life in that book, Nabokov did not simply insert recovered moments into a larger narrative project, studding it with those memory-sensations that had retained their savor and immediacy. He allowed such discoveries to structure the whole enterprise. Scale was everything. Consider: his account of an old friend of his father's, General Kuropatkin, pausing to amuse the child with a handful of wooden matches, takes up more narrative space than the outbreak of war. Of course it does—this was a young boy! But the boldness of that narrative decision astonished me.

And decided me. I admitted what I had denied for so long—that I felt the same way. That the truth of my childhood—or maybe any other part of my life—was often found not in the conventions I used to relay it to others, but rather in these sometimes-odd incidentals. In part because they had not been robbed of their power through explanatory retelling (cf. Proust's madeleine), but also because they really *had* been the occasions of my finest attention. These were the surviving traces of my most private consciousness, and through them some truer picture might be partly reassembled.

This connects, if obliquely, to what I realized during my period of obsessive photo reconnaissance. Going after an image of some Gaudí-esque green pepper (à la Weston), I understood that I was no longer looking at a pepper at all, but a display of contorted surfaces. These, I found, were the true interest, and the fact of its being an edible vegetable was peripheral. I was looking at what William Burroughs had called "the naked lunch," the phenomenological *thing* that he described "quivering at the end of your fork." I was slowly learning to let myself be led by the eye—by what was *there*, rather than what I thought I ought to be looking at.

But important as this felt and was, it was not the real awakening. This conceptual revision was still taking place under the old dispensation. While I was, it's true, increasingly able to see an object or a panorama apart from its function or accepted signification, I was still going to it, seeking it out with some intent. I had not given over being the dutiful photographer, and it was a while before I noticed a certain change in my approach. Nor am I sure how it happened. Was it that I began to trust myself more? Or did I just tire of my dutifulness and somehow find it easier to relent, to give up on making a map before I set forth—much as I've been trying to go mapless for years when putting words on the page?

For as long as I can remember, I've felt the need to bring serendipity into my writing, in terms of both inspiration and process—letting the immediate occasion of the writing, whatever was dictating it, have its part in the expression. I knew that I no longer wanted to write anything that felt like filling out a considered agenda. Some sketched-out consideration is necessary and inevitable, of course—none of us are creatures of pure instinct. But what I had begun to realize was that I was hitting upon connections and insights in the course of the writing that influenced the writing *in the very moment of writing*, modifying the syntax, the tempo of the sentences still being formed.

Clearly the change in process, that willingness to stray from the plan, made a good deal more room for unconscious or preconscious influence. And in giving that influence more rein, was I not siding with the rightness of this other cognition, saying in effect that, yes, the memory of the little game with matches held the deeper truth? Similarly, while taking pictures I felt a growing impatience with my way of going about everywhere as if I had that framing rectangle in front of my face.

Doing this can offer a fresh angle on familiar visuals, and the act of screening identifies the kinds of expectations we bring to the aesthetic. But I found myself bored by deliberate prospecting and increasingly alert to moments of surprise, what I came to think of as double-takes. Walking along, immersed in thoughts, *not* looking, I would suddenly come to attention. At the far edge of my awareness, something was triggering me. It was happening more and more. And this made me consider yet again—it's a long-standing preoccupation of mine—that the instincts, the peripheral reflexes, are quicker and more reactive than the daily navigation system. This time I understood that there was a logical reason for this: because our reflexes are honed toward survival, because they evolved to screen not for the expected thing, but for the anomaly.

In Roland Barthes' *Camera Lucida*, his study of photographs and of looking at photographs, he develops the very useful (and adaptable) concepts of *studium* and *punctum*. (I've mentioned these elsewhere, but I do so again). The former he characterizes as the ostensible subject of the photo, the reason it was taken. The latter, as the word itself suggests, is the little puncture point, the irregularity, the element that doesn't quite fit and which therefore compels the eye and interest. The *punctum* is the unplanned accidental thing that somehow defies the imposed narrative—the misdirected gaze in the class picture, the nervously cocked finger in the official portrait . . .

The *punctum* is the resistance of the real—of the unforeseen—to what has otherwise been foreseen. In this way it is quite similar to the "telling detail" that I'm always going on about with my writing students, the little giveaway clue in some action, the one irregularity that the detective spots in an otherwise airtight alibi. *That* is the true thing. Barthes applied his linked concepts to the existing photograph. *Camera Lucida* is full of illustrative instances: this expression, that small gesture. My move here is to apply them not to the captured images, but instead to the act of perception itself. In this version of things, setting out with a camera to find photographs to take, assaying things in terms of their rightness, their obvious "picturesqueness," would be the *studium* position, while abandoning intent and allowing oneself to be alert and responsive to unexpected pricks or little catches— would be letting the peripheral reflexes make the call. It represents a 180-degree reversal.

Now, though I still go out into the day with my charged-up smartphone in my pocket, things are different. That I carry it with me at all times means I am no longer going about with deliberate intent. I'll have it with me when I'm on an errand, or just walking along. Whatever I'm doing, I let myself lapse as fully as possible into my normal state of distracted reverie, the impulse trail of my thoughts. I do what I have always done, but with this one difference: I have made myself alert to the anomaly, the 'off' detail, for me the visual equivalent of whatever it is that makes a sleeping dog's ears give a sudden vigilant twitch. *What was that?* In most cases it turns out to be nothing, some unexpected discontinuity in the façade of things—a loose candy wrapper on the sidewalk, a flutter of wings off a telephone wire.

Every so often, though, some truly arresting thing pulls me up straight: the sudden hieroglyph of a light post against low rolling clouds, a patch of extraordinary variegated bark, and now and again what I consider a *double* double-take: the utterly immobile profile of a heron in the reeds—the bird itself being the very emblem of the kind of reflex-alertness I'm talking about.

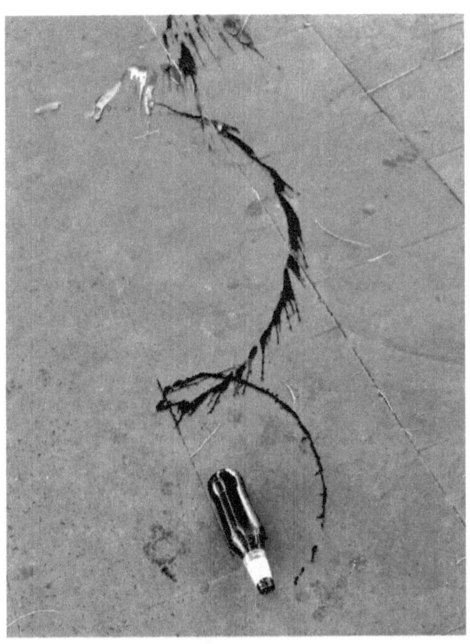

Of course, there is no direct export of recognitions from one art to another, at least not in terms of craft. But there is a kind of psychological permeability. I recognize it sometimes. My hobbyist's play with picture taking has, I think, sharpened my sense of subjective proportion and, for lack of a better term, inadvertency. I feel more attuned to the insight or observation caught on the fly, the stray detail that may prove to be the illuminating thing—and I try to encourage the posture of receptiveness that enables both.

I also feel more convinced than ever that the idea of *should* does not belong in either the making or experiencing of art. *Should* upholds canons, hierarchies, orders of value and importance; it asserts that there is a right way. It seems to me now that the end and origin of both making and experiencing is pleasure. Pleasure in the sense not of easy gratification, but of the true thing hit upon. This sense of pleasure can come from the capture of painful recognitions, too, for the gratification is found not in the subject matter—the *what*—but in some intuitive originality of presentation. This aesthetics, possibly related to Susan Sontag's well-known promotion of erotics over hermeneutics, elevates *punctum* over *studium*, and understands that our unprepared, genuine responses, which obey no canons of "mattering," are the real basis of our connection to the world.

(2015)

Birkerts and I

> *Four years have now passed since it came out in Norway,*
> *and I have traveled around the globe and talked about it*
> *as its translations have appeared in each new country. It*
> *is a soul-devouring task, the division between me and my*
> *literary self being so slight. One thing I know is that I*
> *will never do anything like it again.*
>
> —Karl Ove Knausgård

I'm getting old enough now, and I've spent enough years writing across the spectrum of my various obsessions, that I'm not always sure when I've simply thought something before, when I've tried to work it out in some notebook or even rough draft, and when I've given it a more final shape and actually seen it into print. To go searching back through old pages feels like an admission I don't want to make. I far prefer to think that we all repeat ourselves, and that the saying can deepen with reiteration; and, too, that variations are inevitable—and who among readers remembers anything anyway?

If we were classifying openings, this one might be called preemptive. Remove the possibility of being caught by outing yourself. Make the self-exposure appear a virtue. Introduce your various layerings of ambivalence and ambiguity right away, and let that maneuver serve as your hook.

The other night, turning this way and that in my bed, hoping to get wakeful consciousness to undo itself, I decided I would try writing something in my head, and then I thought about starting this essay. The effort of plotting out sentences, combined with the interiorized drone of my own voice, has often done the trick. With luck I'll get four or five sentences in, advancing the case of something or other, and that will be all. The next thing I know it's morning and I'm listening to the busywork of the birds outside. But alas, on this occasion the self-stupefaction wasn't working. I'd foolishly assigned myself a subject that interests me, and that I've had many thoughts about over the years—authors in their photographs—and, lying there, I could not remember if I had ever written about it at any length, or if I had merely thought about doing so.

This particular uncertainty is, I'll admit, also my way of worrying about memory, subjective record-keeping, and, artistically speaking, about whether it finally matters one way or the other if I have already taken a subject on. After all, writing is, for most of us, a circling around the same basic set of themes, or, switching analogies, a kind of tone-row composition in which we do our best to vary the arrangement of our basic few notes as we go along.

Author photos. Sure, I knew I had written some pages about them. I could think of several riffs right off—one on Walter Benjamin as taken by Gisèle Freund, another on Virginia Woolf posing for the same photographer, but, as I told myself in the throes of those tosses and turns, that didn't matter. What matters is what the writing self wants. The wanting will always find out what it's a wanting *of.* That is the alpha and omega of writing.

~

My fascination with author photos began when I was quite young, more or less coincident with my first real awareness that there were such things as "writers"—people with lives who also wrote books that were, when well done, compelling simulations of life. I was thinking mainly of novels back then. My mother was a great reader of novels, and on occasions when I was alone at home and free to prowl, I would take books from her shelves and study them. Here began the daydreamy worship of graven images, my innocent idolatry.

Of course, the fantasist needs only a prompt, and as my fantasies in those days were about the other life, the life to come—free and non-suburban—I looked first to the adventuring males. Jack London, Hemingway, Steinbeck, Ian Fleming, Thomas Wolfe. The scenarios were stock business: wanderings, struggles, conquests, and great rewards. Indeed, daydreams feast on clichés, but they serve a purpose too. Casting ourselves forward into our imagined futures, we try out designs for the lives we might one day want to live. What steep downward revisions follow.

The study of author photos was a part of that whole enterprise. No mere adjunct or preamble to reading, it was an activity of its own, a specific and delicious hovering between worlds. Here, in the chair by the window, I sat, the would-be reader. There, encoded in the book in my hand, was the other, proxy world—a world I would soon feel stirring to life around me, as vivid as the one I occupied, with its bowls and vases, its ticking refrigerator. And midway between, neither quite here nor there, his status thrillingly indeterminate, was the magician, the Janus-figure who presided. He—at that point in my life the figures were all strong featured men—could claim his spot in the here and now, as the visual image testified; but he also possessed powers of invention that could bring to life those uncanny other realities. I stared, as if by staring I could divine the secret.

This relates, I think, to the common childhood wish for superpowers—and who of us didn't at some point have that imagining? But the analogy is only partial. For I don't mean being able to bend iron bars or send forth sticky threads from the wrist—though those powers have their cachet—but the subtler thrill of having a double being, a hidden special identity always latent in one's daily life.

This doubleness tends to work mainly one way, though. Looking at newsman Clark Kent, bespectacled and unthreatening, you feel the power of what he can become at a moment's notice, whereas you far less often behold Superman and conjure up the bespectacled man in the ill-fitting suit. So it was with these writers and their photos. I would read in the face, the posture, the extraordinary power of creation. Their least thoughts signified. But in a kind of reverse of formula, I also thrilled to think of any of my hero-figures performing ordinary human acts—ordering coffee, buying supplies at the stationers. The tension had everything to do with the distance between worlds, a distance as great as that between mild-mannered reporter and Man of Steel. Which is to say, following my syllogistic way of thinking, writing, or creation of any kind, belonged in the realm of the miraculous. The photos were a reminder, a kind of visual bookmark for this recognition.

In time, I began to assemble my own little collection of household gods. All through college—and, I'm slightly embarrassed to admit, beyond—I curated my various push-pin galleries. Whereas the guys up and down the hall in my freshman dorm could lie back and contemplate the iconic Farrah Fawcett swimsuit poster, or Che Guevara in his beret, I had my pictures of Richard Fariña, J. P. Donleavy, Henry Miller, and D. H. Lawrence. Space was limited and devotions changed, and over time the displacement of one image by another marked out the path of my reading loyalties. Henry Miller gave way to Malcolm Lowry, Fariña was retired and replaced by Julio Cortázar and Blaise Cendrars, and so on.

Pinned above whatever desk I had at the time, these faces were spurs to my own meditations; they reminded me, when homework or day jobs became too oppressive, that the other place existed. I myself had caught little more than the occasional inkling, but these writers clearly knew. And I would let their images point the way to what I saw as their privileged inwardness, a state exempt from ordinariness, charged with special higher seeing.

I was, I see now, confusing the writer's mentality with the best of their achieved work—as if that fought-for expression were for them simply the daily given, as if Lawrence lived every moment in the sensuous key of *The Rainbow*, as if Lowry's every waking perception were as iridescent and dense as his phrases. As time went on, I got a better sense of what that "fought-for expression"—that writing—involved. The activity had almost nothing to do with opening the Yuri Zhivago spigot on a winter's night, or catching words from the air as the movies liked to show. Writing was, with the rarest exceptions, a dance of one step forward and two steps back.

My beginning notion—that there was a sharp divide between the person living the life and the person doing the work—came to seem naïve and somewhat romantic, but I didn't feel I could throw it out entirely. For one thing, plenty of literary testimony supports the view. From Plato's famous banishment of poets from his Republic—that ultimate conferring of power—to Theseus' extraordinary attribution in *A Midsummer Night's Dream* that:

> The poet's eye, in fine frenzy rolling,
>
> Doth glance from heaven to Earth, from Earth to heaven.
>
> And as imagination bodies forth
>
> The forms of things unknown, the poet's pen
>
> Turns them to shapes and gives to airy nothing
>
> A local habitation and a name.

And of course there are Yeats' classic—and unsettling—lines, his either/or, in which:

> The intellect of man is forced to choose
>
> Perfection of the life, or of the work,
>
> And if it take the second must refuse
>
> A heavenly mansion, raging in the dark.

I could go on and on. The belief that artistic perception and impulse are different in every way from the norm is deeply ingrained in the culture.

These days I find that the idea of the split continues to preoccupy me, but less in the absolutist ways suggested by the poets, or in any metaphysical privileging—though the notion of genius still holds sway—and more in leading me to ask how the process, the *doing*, changes the writer over time. Now I think about the great inner exertion, the tuning of the hearing to different sounds, and the focus, which requires a steady effort to suppress the immediate concerns of the day. These cannot but have their effect.

To put the matter in the simplest terms, writing as it draws upon personal experience is a transformative act. Putting one's own experiences and memories into words changes their nature, and I'm not just thinking about memoir. Most literary writing draws on personal material at some level. And this transformative extraction into art alters everything, steadily and cumulatively. The writer doesn't just work at the desk all morning in one psychological mode and then switch it off to walk the dog or go shopping for dinner. There is no simple stepping from room to room—as if only the rooms were different, and the person moving between them was always the same. No, I believe the act of writing changes both the writing "I" and the non-writing "I" in significant ways, and it does this by transforming the basic stuff of subjective identity.

Annie Dillard writes about this very thing in her essay "To Fashion a Text," where she openly asserts, "You can't put together a memoir without cannibalizing your own life for parts. The work battens on your memories. And it replaces them." The expression is so succinct and plainspoken that one could easily read right past it, but those last few words especially have explosive implications. Writing re-wires the psyche—every writer knows this. But, as is so often the case, it has taken time for science to catch up with art. Freud said as much more than a century ago. And so it is—neuroscientists now confirm that the act of recollection affects the brain's organic structure, alters the wiring in measurable ways. The discovery is rich, and it bears quite directly on the question of writerly inwardness and outwardness— and, I think, on my fascination with those photographs, which so directly propose the distinction.

Dillard's observation haunted me for years—long before I'd ever heard of neuroscience—ever since I shifted from writing about books and writers to more personal subjects. Her words aligned with my anxious sense that I was in some way writing myself away from my sources, with every "captured" moment, distancing myself from the original feeling.

What was happening? Harkening to Dillard, the expression in the work was *replacing* what had before been the unstructured stuff of memory. The formulation, like "the letter" in the old adage, killeth the spirit, or whatever it is that the spirit giveth. Meaning, in effect, that by structuring memories and assimilating them to narrative, written expression leaches their affective potency, uses them up. What this suggests, in turn—and much depends, of course, on how fully the writer accesses his material (we are not all of us Prousts)—is that important parts of the writer's life now have their true existence, their incarnation, or sublimation, in verbal form rather than primary sensation. It means that, in a way—half literal, half symbolic—much of the life itself has been moved into the expressive, aesthetically objectified frame, and the writer herself now hovers in a boundary zone between felt and captured emotion.

Tempting as it is to theorize, I don't want to go too far with this, even as I feel more and more that some such core transaction *has* gradually taken place. These days I will call up a memory only to find, strange as this sounds, that the event in question feels less like something I experienced and more like something I read. Which, if I ponder it, is almost accurate. Except that instead of reading it, I *wrote* it—or at least some essential aspect of it. And with this recognition comes a dissociation, one that is somehow both a diminishment— with the loss of the original freshness of the recollection—*and* also an augmentation of the sort that we associate with artistic expression. It's hard to know whether this is good, bad, or one of those things to which those kinds of judgments refuse to adhere.

This primary relation between writing self and other self is the crux of Borges' famous little meditation "Borges and I":

The other one, Borges, is to whom things happen. I walk through Buenos Aires, stop, maybe a bit mechanically, to look at the arch of an entrance way and a grillwork door; I have news from Borges by mail or when I see his name in a list of professors or in a biographical dictionary. I like hourglasses, maps, 18th-century typography, the taste of coffee, and Stevenson's prose; the other shares those preferences but with a vanity that turns them into an actor's attributes. It would be an exaggeration to affirm that our relationship is hostile; I live, I let myself live, so that Borges can plot his literature and that literature justifies me.

It doesn't cost me anything to confess he has achieved a few valid pages, but those pages can't save me, perhaps because what's good no longer belongs to anyone, not even to the other, but to language and traditions. In any case, I'm destined to be lost, definitively, and just some instant of me will survive in the other. Little by little I cede everything, even though I'm aware of his perverse tendency to falsify and pontificate, Spinoza understood that all things want to be preserved in their being: the stone eternally wants to be a stone and the tiger a tiger. I shall remain in Borges, not in myself (if I am someone), but I recognize myself less in his books than in many others and in the laborious strumming of a guitar. Years ago I tried freeing myself from him and went from the mythologies of the arrabal to the games with time and the infinite, but those games are Borges' now and I shall come up with other things. Thus my life is a flight and I lose everything and everything belongs to oblivion, or to the other.

I don't know which of the two writes this page.

As Borges renders it here, this distinction between the individual and the writer is not a split so much as a complex and often tense détente negotiated between divergent realities. The reality of immediate experience—of the man who pauses by the arch of an entryway—as opposed to experience transformed into something projected toward an audience. As writing was said to effectively replace the original memory, taking it out of play in perceptible ways, so, through Borges' speaker, we identify a second sort of interdependence, where the created work gives the individual, the "other Borges," his reason for being.

Borges is a kind of literary mystic, and so we are not surprised that he proposes the created work as more valuable than the contingent life that supplied the necessary materials. But Borges is also at times a sublime ironist, and, no surprise, his same assertion can be read ironically, as if any artistic scribbling could possibly be thought to weigh more than the sublime givens of real living—which are so sublime that they task the feeble artificer with forever trying to reproduce them.

On one of those walls of literary "heroes"—this I remember—I had photographs of both Borges and Hemingway. I thought of them as my polarity figures. Hemingway, all square jawed and hirsute, shown at his typewriter, one finger extended for hunt-and-peck—the only manly way to type, I always thought. He had, I fancied, the look of a

man who could get to his feet without a backwards glance, sling his
jacket over his shoulder, and head out for a night with his cronies.
There was no great division between his realms.

The Borges photo, by contrast, was one of the iconic ones of the
blind old man with his cane—a perfect emblem of double inwardness.
For not only was this the man who spun out the fantastical metaphysical parables—"The Garden of the Forking Paths," "Pierre Menard,
Author of the Quixote"—a master of the most uncanny inward twists
and magnifications—but he was also blind. It seemed perfectly fitting
that he should have written "The Other Borges," for if ever a writer
lived the bifurcation of the two selves, it was this one.

But the self-division I imagined for Borges, and the lack of such
in Hemingway, was probably a young man's faulty and somewhat
clichéd conjuring. I don't know that I judged wrongly of Borges—
his life as ordinary man is not easy to picture. But Hemingway, I'm
now convinced, could not have achieved the quality of his best prose
if he hadn't been capable of sustained feats of dissociative transformation. Those astonishingly vivid renderings of the world—the
Cezanne-inspired efforts at *seeing*—were not done by a man who had
merely paused between fishing a trout stream and decanting another
Bordeaux. My years of experience tell me that no such artistic creation
is possible without the most sustained inward absorption and the
greatest application of pressure on one's material.

This may be why Hemingway's *A Moveable Feast* holds such fascination for me—because it suggests yet *another* paradoxical reverse. I
am, like many, completely taken by the charm of his descriptions of
being young and poor in Paris. The writing is first-rate. But what gives
me pause—happy pause—is the fact that the book was composed late
in the writer's life, at a point when he was deep into alcoholism and, by
his own frequent public admission, tired of things. Be that as it may,
the scenes, as oft-told as they must have been, display the gleam of

freshness, the feel of first exposure. They enact—and celebrate—a connection with memory that would seem to counter everything I've been saying about art depleting its sources and replacing them with words. How could Hemingway have retrieved things so vividly? I can only marvel that he did, and hope—for all of us who write from our lives—that the pull he felt toward his times of greatest happiness, of things most loved, was very strong, and that those experiences were rich enough that even the writer's most intensive labors of mining had not fully exhausted the seams.

(2016)

Scratch

There is sometimes a story in the smallest thing, in the long unraveling scratch of a needle on vinyl, for instance, a sound once so common that we learned to hear right past it, brushing it off as a kind of audial lint, nothing to be bothered by—until we got clean digital sound and started wondering how we had managed to enjoy our music as much as we had, all that fur on our pleasure. I'll go ahead and say, then, piling a mountain of association onto this near-nothing of a base, that it was just that sound, that scratch, that reached me here, in my state, my funk, not to save me—nothing quite so dramatic—but certainly to wake me up to something. Not a big event, as these things go, but on the other hand I have thought of the moment with a tightening sense of connection, so it must mean something, especially since any taste of connection like that has been lacking for a while. I don't know how far back to go. Is this to be my presidential election piece, my *cri de cœur*, my confession of writerly disaffection? It just may be, but if it is, I'll try not to load the meanings on too thickly up front. My point is just that there was a bit of a sound, but that as soon as I heard it I got that verifying pulse of alertness I'm always hoping for, and I knew when the feeling ebbed back that it was, in fact, something bigger.

To try to explain, to set out context, I'll need to push against that strong countering voice ("Stop clearing your throat! Stop piling up those boring lists and explanations!") and narrate to scale—local, domestic—trying to restore the mood of that particular afternoon as I drove to pick up my daughter. My usual late-fall grimness—I certainly had it that day, the feeling that something was skewed in my basic relation to things, that the world I occupy—my version of life—had little or nothing to do with the world on the other side of my windshield. Just witness all those people blowing by me in their SUVs, bleating their business into cell phones. Who were they? I'd been asking it for years, but now I felt more torque in the question. Were *they* the ones who blotted the little ballot balloons with their wrongheaded ink? Was it their fault? So yes, my sense of the outer world was certainly a part of it.

But at the same time—connected to this—I felt the clog of a personal murkiness. The anxious fear that I can't get said what I need to, that I'm no longer clear about where we're going, and that even if I did know, my words would do no good at all. Not just my words, but words in general. I can't help it: when I get into these moods, no matter how I tilt my head, the whole proposition looks dicey. Everything pushes at me: the scatter and distraction of dailyness, the glut of our things, the fact that so few people seem to heed the things I care for. Not just books, but the whole inward-tending way of things. On these darker days I'm absolutely convinced that the idiotic shimmer has taken over, crowding everything else aside to the bright slick thump of some studio-generated piece of feel-good music.

This afternoon, then, my mood is dark and drained, infected by all this spleen, but also by the sudden inability to get my words right on the page, to feel that bright line of connection between thought and expression pulling the self and the world back into balance. Trying to write about my sense of the culture post-election, I've felt reduced to numb, angry generalizations, and, as always happens, the difficulty of getting it right feels like the new permanent condition. On my way to pick up my daughter from school, inserted in the mindless dream-flow of Rt. 128, I flip through my CD case for a sound that might break against all this blandness. Music, my drug, can still work a spell on me at highway speeds—something about the velocity and all that landscape slipping past meshes with the listening state, our looking turning into a kind of thought.

And what I settle on finally—figuring out my mood more through rejection ("no, no, no") than choice—is a mix-CD that a brotherly friend once burned for me, a bouquet of certified heart-breakers, folkie classics, songs I know I can, often enough, burrow my way into. And this time the music, the sequence, does work. By the time I pull up the long school drive and park in my usual spot, I'm in a state, with all my recent frustration and melancholy folded together—the election, my loss of connection, the writing morass, my sense that there are hungry new generations gnawing at our heels—and this state, created and fed by the music, keeps extending itself, somehow growing together with the November darkness that is closing down so swiftly, until finally all things inner and outer seem like part of one plaintive thing. And this, no denying, is the true bottom-line picture of the world. . .

But always, of course—we forget—there has to be the moment of the turn, the shift, when even the cleanest sustained note wears out. This afternoon, in my car in the dark, it comes in the deep quiet that follows the fading out of the song I was listening to—and right after, when I hear that tiny scritching sound. I know my sentimental friend and I recognize the tune, the old British war-time classic "We'll Meet Again"—its crackly, period-piece sadness obviously transferred to CD from vinyl. And right here, with that first bit of audial rustle, I am transfixed, overtaken, almost as if that tiny rasp, that staticky burr, is the forgotten thing I've been in search of all along, and it hits me, if not quite with Proustian force, then still hard, jolting me up, giving me the end of something that can be pulled in or followed.

And there, at the other end—I know this right away, before I even name it—is a very particular time and place. Ann Arbor, thirty-some years ago, with everything in composite: all the little rooms I lived in, upstairs, all the inevitable slanted ceilings, jammed windows, battered wooden fire-escapes, and I have such a strong feeling of those places, their look and stale rankness, everything, my clothes, my posters, my notebooks and piles of papers, my books and my music, the source of it all, that first little stereo I owned that used to manufacture just this hiss I am hearing. Here, in the sound of the ongoing hiss, in the hours and hours of music, morning, afternoon, and night, the tone-arm spiraling down slowly after the last cut of whatever record I have on, then flinging back like a salute to start again—inside all of this, in a jumble, I get the expanding sensation of everything else that was crowded around, not just me, my room, my situation, but also my world, the times themselves, all that feeling we breathed and assumed, the us and the them, the cause, so boldly marked—Nixon and the Pigs here, the people there—all of it together bringing back the future we were pointing at, without even knowing it, when we collected on the street or at long tables in Mark's Coffee Shop or on the Diag, when we knew without question that we were right and that we were next—the same feeling that incredibly, unthinkably, disappeared, stunning us all, leaving us sucker-punched and forced to figure out how to do what-ever had to be done alone, without that solidarity. All those dreamers waking up, everything inexplicably turning, changing, but not before leaving its traces—in the fine-grained details of atmosphere, in the songs, and for me, so I now discover, in the crackle I absorbed without noticing it, those endless few years when I lay on my bed, eyes closed, playing, over and over, my amplified scenarios of the life to come.

(2004)

Drowning

"The pure products of America go crazy," William Carlos Williams wrote, and however he intended that assertion in his poem "To Elsie," I take it here for my own uses. We are drowning—in images, words, everything. I don't know how much we even realize it, such is the abundance and our distractedness in its midst. But the feeling hits me more and more often. Sometimes to the point of sickness: I want to tear a hole in the air in front of me and hurl myself through. Get to some other place, some new Utopia where they haven't thought of all this progress yet—or at least not so much of it. Will I ever find a balance between this relentless crush of signals and the attention needed to do them justice?

I suppose I'm dreaming of some nineteenth-century paradise of the mind, but most likely I've got that all wrong—things were never as I imagined, and somewhere in all the glut are the texts and graphs to prove it.

Not to mention that I am implicated completely. I abet the process every day: generating words, soliciting words, commenting on words. I am busy clogging the ether with my trivia, taking and posting images. To what end? Maybe, convinced as I am of the intransitive nature of the system—how it feeds into chaos and leads nowhere—I should instead be asking: Why do I continue to play the game? Clearly there remains a kernel of faith in the redemptive power of word, of image, of art. It's a hope of exceptionality—the gambler's downfall—that in the face of inundation, even in part *because* of it, I will hit on the expression that acts as a countering spell. More and more, this feels like wishful thinking.

~

It seems I am always gathering evidence, though often I grasp my intent only after the fact. This informal research puts a great deal of trust in the unconscious—that its perceptions or intuitions are ahead of whatever I think I'm thinking about. In the day-to-day I'm just going about my readerly business, looking at books, scrolling through articles that catch my interest, following links to others, occasionally making a note to myself to follow up. But my real allegiance is to serendipity, to a trust in networks of connection between ideas which may not always strike the more logical intelligence. Disparate things can form constellations that only become visible when the sky clears, which is to say when the need is felt, when the right question gets asked. As to what creates the need—what if not the business of living and the soul's demand for meaning?

Here is the most recent instance. It was almost the end of the summer and I was on vacation in the north of Vermont. Though I'd pried myself away from much of the usual business, I was not fully disconnected—is one ever these days? Also, I have to say, I was never not aware that I had an assignment, an essay to be written. To be self-reflexive: this essay. It is so often a task that supplies the necessary tension.

I remember the moment very clearly. I was completely alone on a beautiful lake in a red kayak. It was just dawn, and I was being both romantic and dutiful—a familiar oxymoronic state. Paddling, watching the strokes make clean cuts in the water, I was trying to heed Dr. Williams' prescription of "no ideas but in things." And failing. I just could not get the better of myself. I had come to the very center of natural beauty and suddenly I was having ideas. I was thinking, focusing on two separate words. They had come to me—spoken distinctly from self to self—as the leading edge of a chain of association I had not been aware of following. The words were *intention* and *uniqueness*.

How can I describe what a clear signal they gave me? Because, when they arrived, I thought quite pointedly: "Here is my beginning!" And: "I have to look them up, find their roots."

I had been gathering evidence, I saw that right away. Reading along the lines of inclination (and who will ever explain how that works?), I had also been tagging things in that half unconscious way—not just willy-nilly, but with some intuition of eventual usefulness. Now, as I moved over the water, I caught the inner glimpse of some of my sources: an essay in *The Nation* about Instagram, various short pieces from a new book by Teju Cole, and an essay I'd just finished by Cynthia Ozick. They clustered in my mind, marking out a perimeter. They defined the area I wanted to think inside. The two words were a gift—my keys, my goads.

~

The Nation article, by Ricky D'Ambrose, is entitled "Instagram and the Fantasy of Mastery." I'd picked it up a few months before, probably because I'd recently begun to dabble with Instagram myself, using it to store certain pictures I'd taken—a most limited use of what I knew to be a sophisticated technology. And in fact a good part of D'Ambrose's essay is about Instagram's extraordinary digital palette and the choices it gives the user. He writes about the ingenious range of our various iPhone photo apps—how these now allow, even *encourage*, the picture taker to create a "look." A look, as D'Ambrose uses it here, is a styled visual product that draws on a range of formerly innovative, and now menu-ready, artistic effects. Now everyone can use the various filters and preset templates and, D'Ambrose asserts, be an "artist."

I read with interest, but for me there was a larger implication—that something at the core of making, disseminating, and evaluating images has changed. Not just the fact of people flooding our collective visual space with their iPhone photos, but also how this might affect our view of Art and its place in the human order. D'Ambrose is not the first to make many of these points, but his reflection came right as I'd been worrying the whole question of inundation.

While D'Ambrose's focus is mainly on the visual, his observations are clearly relevant to all the expressive arts. "Something becomes interesting," he writes, "when it can be separated out from an immense crowd of similar objects. . . . It's what happens when art becomes a token of 'visual culture,' or is absorbed into the undifferentiating and deathless vertical scroll of digital images. When the eye must, in one critic's words, 'rapidly target relevant data in a noisy stream,' or when the worth of a picture is a function of how attractively it registers on a screen, being interesting is the preferred (and perhaps only) criterion of declarable value. And one way of making an image interesting—the quickest, most seductive way—is by furnishing it with a look."

The key word here, for me, is "furnishing"—for it conveys the sense of adding on, of supplying something in a decorative, not originating, manner. In an arts culture in which so much—if not nearly everything—has been done and said, the issue is not so much one of invention, but of renovation—of finding ways to sustain interest, which is to say create the sense of novelty and relevance. D'Ambrose's point is that we now have tools (apps, etc.) that have been designed so that we can create the "look" that gratifies artistically. But what happens when that "noisy stream" increasingly comprises these "interesting" images? We keep upping the stakes—what can anyone express that will stand out against everything around it?

Interest is tied here to uniqueness, though this is a uniqueness achieved by virtue of standing out, being different from what surrounds—uniqueness that takes the form of a negation, a *not* being like everything else. This is very different than the uniqueness that results from invention, a fresh expression not seen before. But how likely are we to find such in a world where most everything has been done and re-done? This is the maker's crisis in a nutshell. D'Ambrose reflects on how much the calculated appearance depends on the appropriation and combination of elements from the prior work of others. The "creative" (his name for the contemporary producer) now "ransacks a thin chronology of images . . . ready to recover from everything before him the most potentially exciting look—his salvageable loot—that Canon or Apple can engineer."

What kept D'Ambrose's essay in my thoughts were its wider implications about originality and interest—and uniqueness and intention—in the face of our unprecedented level of visual signal. These I found amplified by a number of Teju Cole's essays. Cole is a critic keenly aware of the new context of the digital—the changed access, and new modes of production—and how it puts new pressure on the idea of the aesthetic. His essays, gathered in *Known and Strange Things*, center on photography, but radiate in all directions.

Cole's focus in several of the photography-themed essays is on the mix-and-match scavenging aesthetic that is such a natural consequence of visual overflow. For now, alongside the fantastic temptation of available images, we have technologies engineered to gather and process them in endless ways. This processing testifies to the exhaustion of previous styles—there seems to be little seeing that is not in some way a response to predecessor work. After Post-postmodernism, what?

In the essay "Finders Keepers," Cole considers various artists who draw their material directly from the internet's digital cataract, culling and combining. The artist, he notes, plays a revivifying role. For internet images (which these days comprise nearly all images) are "vulnerable . . . to the dual threats of banality and oblivion—until someone shows up, says 'Finders keepers,' rethinks them, and by that rethinking, brings them back to life." Expression here becomes an act of re-contextualization, a process which is theoretically endless.

Artists and photographers now obviously exert a good deal of energy on this resuscitation. When the world-surface is layered over with images, copies, and commentary, what else is there to draw on? Is it even possible for the would-be maker to see the old world in back of the imagined edges of this accumulation? The new given is less and less the primary world, ever more a referential one.

Whether these initiatives are the same as invention is another question. I would say not. While invention also draws on prior materials—the world as the artist finds it—it also insists on the terms of its singularity. Scavenger art—art drawing on prior image culture—while often thoughtful and provocative, is more commentary than fresh assertion, a kind of midrash on the world of signs.

Cole's essay "Google's Macchia," begins with his astonishment at Google Image search, and goes on to ponder its underlying algorithm, which works with something called "macchia." Macchia are minutely codified visual elements that can be used to identify affinities among what are often surficially dissimilar images—"a woman with a hijab was now surrounded by her color patch relatives: a fighter jet, Bill Maher being conspiracy weary. . . ." Mere appearance is often trumped by other similarities—of structure, tonal variation, and so on. Cole wonders what this might portend for our image-makers. It creates new possibilities for relating thing to thing, no question. But the door is now also open to connections no longer based on the artist's own subjective recognitions—literal patterns or metaphoric insights—but rather on calculations derived from codified bits. We can think of these bits as extracted visual DNA, and the process itself as something akin to cloning.

"The Atlas of Affect," surveys several artists working with found images, including Dina Kelberman. Her ongoing project, *I'm Google*, is based on an ongoing Google Image search, and plays with a core ambiguity—whether the images in question were assembled by a human sensibility or a randomized bot. Looking up the project, we scroll through what feel like virtual reams of kindred thumb nail images: balloons, people in marching formation, beach-sand constructions . . . It is impossible not to wonder what the point of such accumulation is—and, naturally, what kind of selection criteria were imposed. Cole calls what she is doing "a kind of reverse Turing test." Is this a human organization, and if it is, to what purpose are these images brought together?

This may be a special instance within a subset of art making, but for me it feels like a warning, one that happens to relate to both of my keywords. A work premised on the arrangement of internet images obviously counters any conception of individualized "making"— though any non-algorithmic act of selection presupposes a selecting sensibility, and therefore an agenda. But the fact that we don't know whether it was an individual or a program making the choices complicates the game. If it is a program, then the project becomes a statement about that fact. If we are left to wonder, on the other hand, then it has become a referendum on intention.

Intention is one of the foundation stones of our idea of art: that the created thing has a maker and a purpose. Of course, there are myriad exceptions and variations: collectively originated performances and improvisations, OuLiPo documents that fulfill arbitrarily generated constraints, and so on. But the driving assumption of Western art of the last centuries, summed up by Ezra Pound's modernist injunction to "Make it new," is of original creations—beautiful or meaningful (or both)—that also reflect our march forward in time. If we consider many of the works from our current image culture, however, we might begin to think that that particular script is nearly used up. We

are waist-deep in image and text—our pure products going crazy—
and the making and experiencing of art has to be changing.

~

Walter Benjamin's "The Work of Art in the Age of Mechanical
Reproduction," a standard reference in the debate on originality—
which now might read "The Work of Art in the Age of Digital
Transmission"—proposed that an "aura," a kind of emanation of
its created authenticity, inhered in the unique, made thing, and was
cancelled out by its being replicated and distributed. Has digitiza-
tion taken it all further? Possibly not as concerns painting, but with
photography it has struck directly at the root. Code has replaced the
physical trace—with the result that there is no distinguishing between
original and full-resolution copy: there is only the original, no matter
how many clones are made.

Evolving technology has changed things in the larger frame as
well. For one thing, most encounters with art now happen at a remove,
mediated and multiplied by screens or swathed in volumes of link-
driven info-hype. Going to a live event—rock concert, opera, boxing
match—all too often means watching it as a real-time big-screen tele-
cast where what is lost in immediacy of presence is compensated by
better visibility. Movies, as we know, have migrated significantly to
home-view, with all the benefits of pause, replay, and so on. Books
take up residence on reading devices of all descriptions.

This transformation affects the maker's conception of audience
and the audience's conception of the work. The pressures of proliferation, ready simulation, open access (I mean: Youtube, Netflix,
Instagram, and all their kindred), not to mention the psychological
fact of the felt adjacency of all "information," have contaminated
our experience of the read, heard, watched, or seen thing. This last,
the "felt adjacency" of everything—texts, music, visuals—is not an
easy concept to formulate, though it works on us incessantly, obey-

ing the basic principle of inflation, which is the lessening of value by the heightening of availability. In our role as "consumers of information"—the phrase says it all—we buy our bread with bushels of depreciated currency.

A copy is by definition a redundancy—but when redundancy attains a certain critical mass it becomes something else. It becomes *saturation*. Saturation quite literally means that the receiving body cannot easily absorb more. The information, the art, can no longer leverage its former effect because the circuits won't accept it. Saturation has made it ever more difficult for us to attend to most anything. In the arts, where engagement is everything, an expression has to seize the interest of the viewer/reader quickly, or else the battle is lost. In my kayak, I suddenly fastened on the words *uniqueness* and *intention*, but what I was really thinking about, I see now, was this reality of there being just too much of everything.

~

These various developments—replication, sampling, and saturation—make the old question inevitable: *What makes something art?* Also: *What happens to art when no one is paying attention?* Changes in the work and its transmission are bound to affect our understandings and valuations.

It was this thorny issue of value that brought Cynthia Ozick into my thinking. As staunchly conservative as her position is, and as literary as her preoccupations are, her work brings up questions that are relevant—and pressing—across the spectrum of all the arts.

In an earlier time, before digital culture prevailed, there existed a set of aesthetic definitions as well as a recognizable system of filters—the so-called critical establishment. This establishment, largely sponsored and supported by the pre-digital media, comprised a population of critics and reviewers, some on official payroll, others freelance, and many of the latter with clear connections to the academic establishment. They were the arbiters of quality, and quality was assessed in terms of various accepted understandings. This is the familiar gate-keeper issue, and Ozick brings it forward again in her newest book, *Critics, Monsters, Fanatics, and Other Literary Essays.*

In her essay "The Boys in the Alley, the Disappearing Readers, and the Novel's Ghostly Twin," Ozick decries the rapid decline of print journalism, which, she holds, is a direct result of the ascendancy of digital media. Screen culture has atomized what was once a thriving critical establishment, destroying the public arena in which value and merit were contested by bona fide critics. Responsible taste-making, as she describes it, has been replaced by a chaos of opinion outlets, everything from blogs to unrefereed Amazon commentaries. Ozick does not worry whether the novel itself will survive. "The next Saul Bellow may at this moment be playing patty-cake in his crib," she quips. What she's distressed by is what is *not* happening. "What is not happening is literary criticism." Simple as that. The critics are gone—they have died off or gone into academe. Ozick rues what she sees as a great defection of talent from the job at hand. With fewer venues, and fewer voices, we are losing the sense of cultural context on which the flourishing of literature (and all the arts) depends.

Though this assessment has the status of received wisdom in certain quarters, I would beg to differ, to propose that Ozick might have things backwards. It is not the lack of critics that is responsible for the collapse of context, but rather the collapse of context that has—even more than the disappearance of venues—undermined the status of the critic. The kind of context, or coherence, that Ozick is asking for is all but impossible to discover now. We are living—behold the evidence everywhere around us—in what writer G. W. S. Trow once called "the context of no context." As the proliferating tech-nologies and expanded venues for self-expression all but guarantee saturation, so the shattering of comprehensible contexts defeats the ambitions of critics who might have served them.

~

I have felt this sense of being untethered for years, and feel it now more than ever. Historically speaking, the transition to digital culture has been a finger-snap. For me, personally, it has coincided with—and more or less defined—my experience as a critic and reviewer. I came of age in what I feel now was the last phase of the old dispensation, and the changes of the last two decades have completely rewritten my expectations and practice. There is obviously no question of things going back to the status quo ante—the structure of the system has changed too much. There will be no rebirth of Ozick's late-lamented center. As the arts have been balkanized, so has the discourse around them. The question, underscored, is "what now?"

Though, once again, maybe that's the wrong question. Are we bound to think in terms of a sequential *next* development? Is the concept of a forward moving arts culture reflecting a forward-moving society even viable? Maybe such timeline constructions are—like the question *What is art?*—themselves a product of less-fragmented eras. We now inhabit an open and overpopulated artistic field, one in which every sort of initiative looks to claim a place. Is there any imaginable common ground?

I do think of one thing. Which is that as we move away from those former ideas of art and progress, we will very likely find the process marked by nostalgias of every description. Less maybe the specifics of what was, more the feeling of its rapid and turbulent loss. The past does not give way quite *that* easily. New surfaces may shimmer, but the old, the former, is implanted everywhere in our language, our rituals, and our cultural myths. And so are our emotions. Will they not have their release?

These nostalgias, though I don't know exactly how to define or characterize them, will not be trivial. Indeed, they may greatly influence what happens. I'm not talking about a retro reprocessing of the images and icons of the past—that already happened with the flourishing of postmodernism. I suspect—and hope—that we'll see something more searching and valedictory, an expressiveness bearing all the markings of our new era, but suffused with feeling, both of homage and mourning.

Who can guess the forms the next expression will take? I can't. But whatever they are, they will represent a very distinctive kind of progress.

(2016)

Semblance: Something Else Again

—Charles Baudelaire

Last month, the night before heading to the Midwest for a big family wedding, I hopscotched around with the remote (remember when there were dials?) and finally landed on *56*, the most recent installment of *Up*, Michael Apted's ambitious serial documentary project tracking the lives of fourteen British children, beginning in 1964, when they were seven, and revisiting them every seven years. This was the eighth installment, with Apted having directed every one of the films after the first, *Seven Up!*. I have by now seen most of the films, not in sequence as one might ideally, but in a hit-or-miss fashion, *stumbled* upon—as happened this time as well.

But linear consistency doesn't matter so much here. For one thing, how many of us have the cine-visual memory to keep that much biographical material straight? For another, it's part of Apted's method to liberally interpose clips from the earlier films into each new portrait segment, so that we see not only the more upholstered and prosperous 56-year-old in her—or his—setting, but also that same person as a child on the school playground, as a teen in a nightclub, young and married, a new parent. It would be very hard to watch any of the eight films without becoming, at least for the duration, a student of fates, a philosopher.

How fitting, then, that my most recent bout of semblance angst should have been triggered by Apted. *Semblance angst*—that's my name for the immediate inner disquiet I feel when the sight of one face suddenly calls to mind another that I can't identify; it's like having a word on the tip of my tongue, but amplified many-fold. There is active unrest until the match is made. I know, of course, that my response is completely out of proportion to the ostensible cause. Why should I care that the thin man sitting opposite me on the subway looks like someone I think I used to know, or have seen on some detective show? Making the right match should not matter to my day, at least no more than does finding the word with the right number of letters to let me finish my crossword. But—

In this case, as I said, I was watching *56 Up*, completely absorbed in the present-day circumstance of one of the subjects, a man who seemed to have done quite well for himself. I paid close attention to the clips, contemplating as is inevitable the physical changes brought by time, and making some not-all-that-refracted references to the comparable points along my own curve. This can't be avoided. Any general witnessing of the works of time is also taken personally; it's human nature. As Jim Morrison said: "No one here gets out alive."

But I didn't have a chance to start a full-dress inventory, for the scene shifted. The man was now sitting on a modern couch beside a thin, attractive, tightly coiffed woman. A second wife, a new partner? I'd somehow missed the voice-over segue and the relationship wasn't clear. But who she was to him didn't really matter to me. What registered just then, in the flash of first impression, was her face. And then the whole familiar business. No use my dismissing it as trivial and trying to put it out of mind. The fret was on. Who did she look like? Who? Who?

I was watching the show with my wife, Lynn, who herself can sometimes get caught up by this chasing of likeness. I asked her if she had it, too, the "she looks just like" agitation. But hers was not a satisfying reaction. "Maybe, yeah—someone . . ." Was she humoring me? Clearly this face was not triggering her in the same way. The shuffling and sorting was going to be all up to me.

First, as always, I scanned for associations, tried to determine if this was a face I knew from my own immediate experience, or one from some other context. Movies, television, magazines? I couldn't say. You'd think the line between firsthand exposure and secondary media would be fairly distinct. But I had no sense either way—the image pool was without category distinctions. It was maddening. Next I tried to bear down inwardly on what those features signified. What affect, what vibration? I watched the segment attentively, waiting for the lens to find her again. If I could only pause the thing and study the arrested frame. But there was no way. On the scale of human vexation this was minuscule, but the obsessive mind does not think of scales. Who *was* she? Cool, thin, skin drawn tight over the cheekbones, in every way "put together"? Who matched that description?

And then, alas, the time was up. The man's segment, his Warholian interlude, was done. Just like that, the camera angles changed—different sounds, a new background. The next segment was up, and my attention shifted to take it in. Such is the seducing, seam-erasing power of narrative. All I needed were a few establishing images and I was caught up in new comparisons and surmises. The mystery was forgotten.

Except, you see, it wasn't. Indeed, the whole point of this narration is to get me to the moment two days later, when I'm sitting in an outdoor chair by a lake in Nebraska with Lynn and several of her brothers and sisters. The afternoon is warm and sunny, the conversation meandering. I am tuning in and out, pleasantly adrift, when I suddenly experience the unexpected—and deeply gratifying—sensation of hook-finding-eyelet—separated elements connecting, closure. Like that, out of the blue. Nothing could have been further from my mind—though I realize this is a figure of speech, as most other things were just then equally far—which is to say *not at all* in my thoughts. Stretched out there in that chair, in my spot in the shade, I said, at first only to myself, "Joan Allen."

As I said the name I felt a ripple of private delight. Joan Allen. Joan Allen, the actress who played Pat Nixon, who was also in the movie *Pleasantville*. Joan Allen, whose face I have stared at with special raptness because it is so compelling. How was it that I didn't get it right away? But never mind, the woman in the documentary was the *very image* of Joan Allen. And so pleased was I, and so convinced that this meant something, that I waited and waited for a pause in the conversation, and when it finally came I looked at Lynn and said, "Joan Allen." Which I knew would just then mean nothing to her, but which I had to say anyway. "Joan Allen—the woman in that show the other night." As if I then expected her to get up and do a little dance. "You know, the show?" Never mind.

This could all stop here, with a bemused remarking of one of the coincidences of daily life—*I was just thinking of you when you called!*—or it could take a small speculative next step forward, conjecturing about our inevitable attributions to likeness, and what our various tip-of-the-tongue experiences suggest about how the mind works. But as it happened—and of course I see this as purposeful—these very themes were brought to intensified focus a short time later by another, to me far more uncanny, exposure. Do certain kinds of events come in series? Or is it that we find ourselves tuning in to them only when our psyches are at some particular state of readiness?

The other evening, intrigued by a reference in a book I was reading, I searched YouTube for clips from the BBC documentary filmmaker Adam Curtis. There was quite a selection—I was surprised—so without taking too much time to investigate my options, I clicked the link for a film called *The Trap: What Happened To Our Dreams of Freedom?* A few minutes in, I was completely broadsided. Curtis, I've since learned, likes to work in a quasi-collage format, interspersing his more straightforward documentary footage with odd, at first glance anomalous, bits. Early in *The Trap*, clearly spoofing for comic relief, he has inserted a clip from what appears to be a thirties British movie. Black-and-white and a bit grainy and rough in the way that old film gets. We see a jowly, pompous professor type lecturing an unseen audience. He is strenuously underscoring something about human differences, men and women—the sexes—and after holding on his face for a moment, the camera pans around to reveal a classroom full of well-dressed public-school boys at their desks. And there, looking over at me from the back row, is my nineteen-year old son, Liam. What name are we supposed to give to a split-second version of a tectonic shift?

What I register here is the stroke of the uncanny. I do a double-blink, a head-shake; and then I scroll back. For an irrational moment I am not thinking, 'He looks like Liam,' but *Liam!* How quickly, then, the rationalizing revision is accomplished: there is someone in an old movie who looks like my son. I click the arrow. This next time through I will confirm that what's in the clip is not quite what I registered, too this or too that. Such is the usual way of things. We have a flash, then we adjust. I watch again, and this time I am completely tuned in, alert as a hunter, leaning way forward, ready to pounce, and when the camera shifts from the face of the stuffed shirt to the shot of his audience, I am ready to hit pause, and I do. And by God, there he is again! My son, Liam, looking over from the desk by the window, no question. The hair, face, mouth, the facial expression, even, I'm thinking, that elusive thing we call "aura," that *je ne sais quoi* . . . I pause, breathe in, breathe out. No question. Which is to say: if I didn't know better . . .

Well, what am I to do here? Some kind of corroboration is wanted. And for that I have to wait—I'm home by myself. But when my son drops by the house a few hours later to pick up some things he needs, naturally I ambush him as he comes in the door. It's all I can do to get him to sit down without giving myself away. Obsessives are funny this way. I want his straight reaction, I want to see if he sees it.

Finding the video takes me several moments, but then I have it, and he bends in while I pull myself slightly back. I'm watching him in profile. And when the camera pans over to the boys in the classroom, I see him smile. He sees it. I'm not crazy! He clicks it back himself, watches again. Smiles again. "Wow," he says at long last, "that *does* sort of look like me, doesn't it?" That's it. He exhales a single laugh and stands up.

What was I expecting? *That* would be the question—in both instances. That a woman in a British documentary should look like the American actress Joan Allen is a completely trivial happenstance; so is the fact that a schoolboy in a thirties movie looks so very much like my son. The alphabet of features is finite, as is the range of their basic placement on the face. Doublings, echoes, puns—they are inevitable. Everyone knows this. There is a whole entertainment sub-genre premised on this: the Marilyn Monroe clone, Key West's annual Ernest Hemingway look-alike competition. That sub-genre does depend, however, on our collective fascination with this fact, the recognition of improbability—what are the odds of one person looking just like another?

They're low, but they exist. End of story. Again, you would think. Except that no—there's more. For these two recent flashes have now called up something else, and I can't quite let the matter rest. A short time ago, while writing notes for this, I found myself remembering a moment from this past spring. I had obviously tamped it down. But now, following Freudian protocol, it was back, a little vignette.

On my way home from work one April afternoon I had stopped into our local wine shop, as I do a few times a week. The woman behind the counter, who I've come to be on nodding terms with, gave me a strangely searching look and then, when I approached the register, asked, "Were you by any chance in here a little while ago?" I shook my head. "I was working," I said. "Are you sure?" she persisted. I gave her a look. It was clear she only half believed me. She was staring at me now, mock suspicious, and I could feel her taking me in feature by feature. There was a long pause, which she finally broke by saying, "I swear . . . there was a guy and he looked just like you." I didn't know what the right response would be. I said nothing, made a wry slow-motion shrugging gesture.

But in truth, I was more disconcerted than bemused. What did this mean? Here was a woman who sat in her quiet shop all day, who could not help but look at people, and who clearly *did* take note of who came through the door, who certainly knows what I look like. She was a credible witness. But what did it mean that she fingered me in this way?

I think of myself as having a somewhat odd—that is to say *distinctive*—physiognomy, but maybe everyone feels that about themselves. We are, all of us, self-embedded, wrapped up entirely in our sense of personal uniqueness, the sign of which is our physical appearance, most immediately the face. Does anyone think that he or she is ordinary—repeatable? To be sure, I allow that there are others in the world, a few, who might, from a certain distance, look like me. But *from a certain distance* and *in the world*. From the selection pool of billions. Not here in Arlington, Massachusetts, where we would be drawing on a mere few thousand. *That* thought chafed.

Sitting in the car, I waited a bit before starting up. Other things were now getting to me. One was the obvious extrapolation. If what the woman at the counter had remarked was true, if there really was that "I swear" resemblance, then people all over town could be seeing my ostensible double and thinking it was me. Or else seeing me and thinking I was the other person. What were the implications? I could feel myself starting to obsess. The implications would, of course, depend on the character, the presentation, of the other. If he was mild and restrained—as I fancy myself to be—then maybe no great matter. But if he were, say, obnoxious, snide, high-handed . . . I could not begin to work through the possibilities.

More existentially unsettling, though, more angst-inducing, was the other question. In what ways, and just how far, did likeness bleed together with character? Surely it was more than a matter of surfaces. An appearance, a look, is not a given, something presented at birth *full stop*. Appearance is edited and edited again—watching Apted's series gave evidence of that. To use another metaphor: the features may be dealt from the deck, but the facial identity is the playing out of the hand. A person's look is the product of years, decades, of expressions, grimaces, habitual movements; it comes to reflect—summarize—all of any person's emotional responses, ways of being. The body cannot but manifest the nuances of the inner life, at least when contemplated at close range. If someone were truly my physical doppelgänger, wouldn't there have to be other shared attributes as well? Imagining the next scenario, the heart-stopper, was inevitable: that I should one fine day round the corner and come face to face with myself.

So distressing was the whole business, the tangle of implications, that I finally just set it all aside. I gave my head a clearing shake, started the car, and drove right back into my unique, singular life. And honestly, I did not think about the episode again until I started writing, which I was prompted to do after I had spotted that shimmering ectoplasm in the back row of a public school classroom.

The question of semblance is now live for me. What exactly *is* our investment in the particularity of our appearance? Is there a person anywhere who wants to hear that he or she looks just like somebody else? Myself, I don't feel multiplied or enriched by the thought of another—or, God forbid, *others*—who look like me. I feel reduced, suddenly one of a set. But neither is this simply about the desire for uniqueness. Resemblance—the repetition of semblance—forces the issue: whether there is in fact some relation, some accord, between the inner being—character, nature—and the outward appearance. Our features mostly do declare our habitual expressiveness. Even the nuances of restraint, emotion held in check, leave their traces and can be discerned. But then, on the other hand, there is no foolproof key of equivalences. And exceptions are inevitable. We know that sometimes the most volcanic temperaments are masked by bland impassivity, and that the wiliest operators give every appearance of mild ingenuousness—doing so is their stock-in trade. Among the roster of publicized Hemingway look-alikes we would very likely find the full range of personality types.

So why do I find myself so vexed and intrigued, so *haunted*, by these instances? Joan Allen! That tousle-headed sixth former! For God's sake. But it's true, every time I remark a human likeness I feel myself quicken: there is something in the wind. What is it? I have no special interest in Joan Allen or the partner of the man in *56 Up*. My interest—it's coming clear to me now—is in the recurrence of likeness itself. Not approximate likeness or mere similitude—close-calls and types mean nothing to me. I'm talking about a match that feels exact. It's rare, but when it happens there is the sounding of a harmonic—a distinct vibration running through the order of things.

What I'm talking about is, I recognize, a species of coincidence. Indeed, it *is* coincidence, except that instead of having a circumstance in which two otherwise independent events are linked by meaning, this is about two unrelated faces achieving overlay in the mind. That overlay suggests a possibility of connectedness, or kinship, outside the sphere of what logic will allow. It does not make an argument for it—and couldn't, any more than could coincidences or Jung's creaky arguments for synchronicity.

But I'm not after proof. Instead, what I feel myself responding to is a kind of happy surplus, and it brings a reminder that we all preserve in ourselves vestiges of primitive "magical thinking," synaptic traces not yet snuffed out by the long millennia of evolution—nor, in certain populations, even close to being snuffed out. I'm thinking right now of all those who still trek to shrines, discern features in shrouds, say their rosaries . . .

But I get off track when I bring up religion, which *is* different. The vigilance I'm remarking is secular, and my inklings do not bring me one step closer toward the mentality of the religious. I am, rather, on the watch for resonances to be found in the immediate stuff of existence and that do *not* betoken any idea of gods or a God. Sightings of exceptional resemblance, along with certain coincidences, touch off sensations in me like what I experience during certain vivid dreams—sensations of being just on the verge, certain for the moment that daily life is just a shadow thrown by something else again.

These are eye-beam shimmers and peripheral intimations, and most likely, along with adrenaline aggression and the flight reflex, nothing more than the last resilient traces of the species' former ways. But even so—or maybe for that very reason—I would not want to think that over further eons we will evolve past them altogether. For these feelings allow us to cast doubt on what we could so readily accept as a world ruled by explicable and rationalized behaviors. The uncanny testifies, if only faintly now, to whatever it is that keeps us making and seeking to experience art. We still want to believe that there are sensations of connection that our breathtakingly complex technologies can't offer us, vibrations elicited not by the futuristic present, but by things that go back even beyond recollection.

(2013)

The Ghost of Electricity:
The Dylan Face

I remember how I used to shake my head when the literary theorists of the 70s and 80s started in on their semiotic analyses, all that business about 'signs' and 'referents.' I found it such a strange way of looking at the world, but I could also see a kind of sense in it. And for a time I did my best to follow along. It was the intellectual order of the day, after all. Everything was a language, a millrace of competing codes. I drew the line, though, at the 'transcendental signifier,' that anchoring entity that supposedly gave meaning to everything else in the relativistic slipstream, but which for me toppled straight into absurdity when Lacan, I think it was Lacan, linked it to the primacy of the phallus, that symbolically vertical entity that could be seen to preside over certain discourse like a conductor's baton, with everything falling in behind it. Find that phallus and arrest the chaotic flow. I'm sure it was more nuanced than that.

Fashions fade, of course. Years have now passed without anyone using the words 'transcendental signifier' in my presence. It arrived of its own accord the other day, hard on the heels of my first of several viewings of Martin Scorsese's recent documentary "No Direction Home." I know how ridiculous that sounds, but isn't a great deal of our thinking absurd at the point of germination? I was trying to get clear from a blue tangle that I'd managed to wrap myself in—I'd gone from wanting to write some simple responses to Scorsese's portrait to experiencing a total mental saturation. And how not? The whole of my affective interior is cross-hatched with Bob Dylan. I was sixteen when I was first bowled over by "Don't Think Twice, It's Alright," and I'm almost seventy when writing this. Though there have been gaps of attention and devotion, I've never strayed far from the music or the lore. Lines from his songs are woven through my whole memory grid. There was, I realized, no standing to one side to make an assessment. Nor has there ever been a clear emblem figure to make an assessment *of*. From the first, Dylan's career has been a procession of masquerades, brilliant stylized poses, reversals—in fact, the very *point* of Dylan, at some level, has been this mercurial game.

What I had with Dylan—I sensed this watching—was a teeming swirl of signifiers overlaying a veritable jungle of signifieds, the whole great mass of images and words sliding around, as signifiers are said to do, with my own identifications everywhere adding to the complication. I saw no way to find purchase and address the whole business directly. Not that I didn't try—I scribbled pages of notes, doing everything I could to boil chaos down to some version of 'first principles.' But nothing firmed up, nothing clicked together like I liked things to click. And then, suddenly, ironically, I got that phrase in my ear, and for the first time I was able to step to the side of my own fussing. Enough, at least, to realize that all along I'd been asking myself, the mind's needle skipping in a circular groove, why I was so interested, so *compelled*, by one particular aspect of Scorsese's film, by the intercut segments of 'present day' footage of Dylan responding to questions.

The obvious answer was that deep down I'm a rubbernecker who is drawn to all sites where Time has been doing its work. *Of course* I would be fascinated to study the man as he looks now, to move my loupe over the features of Joan Baez's "original vagabond." But, absorbing as I found the aging face, its lines and pouches, its repertoire of expressions, it was not the spectacle of change and continuity that held me so much as the startling realization that here, for once, through design or happy chance, I felt like I was seeing the face behind the mask—unadorned, without its thousand protective feints, sans its veils of sarcasm, its obfuscation, its deliberated elusiveness. Just a man talking—unless of course, and I thought of this right away, this was the ultimate performance of them all. But I don't think so. I've seen the film three times now, and the shock of those segments is still acute. They are nothing in themselves, simple headshots of a famous artist talking, pausing, fumbling to articulate his responses. Absolutely everything is found in the contrast. And it is when I watch these recent segments that I get, profoundly, what I've always sensed: that from his first filmed appearances Dylan was never that. Never not posing. Not even in his most 'authentic,' unwashed, scraggly 'troubadour' days. He was—I theorize—always Robert Zimmerman, trick-or-treating, donning the garb of the wanderer, the hard-luck Woody Guthrie, or the lyric surrealist—those myriad identities that Scorsese has soldered together. This, for me, is the disturbing draw of the film. Without these cut-in segments I would be watching just another well-done documentary, following the familiar hagiographic trail that starts with the early still photo images of childhood and family, then moves to interviews with aging survivors—friends, fellow musicians— everything held together with generous lengths of concert footage. An interesting portrait in itself, but nothing like the revealing artifact Scorsese has put together.

From the first, Dylan's core dynamic—the dynamic established and certified by his decision to change from being five-syllable Robert Zimmerman to plain Bob Dylan—has been his exuberant will to impersonation, the creation and maintenance of a public self that is not only seen as ever-changing but is at the same time always at a slant to any expectations his listeners might have. Naturally, this is just the outward play of guises, his mock-serious theater, a vastly heightened version of what many of us do at certain times in our lives. Something more than impersonations, but less than incarnations, these shifts of presentation would be merely interesting if it were not for the music which is, so often, so obviously, profound—arguably the most important musical oeuvre of our time. I don't think I have to list songs, or quote phrases and lines and verses, to make my case.

Normally I run on two tracks with Dylan. Listening to the music I tend to forget the shape-shifting of the public phenomenon. Almost any one of his great lyrics goes straight to the inner man, giving me an artistic connection that renders the idea of such gamesmanship almost incidental. Only on the other track, watching the film, do I confront the icon and feel the palpable tension between levels. This tension expresses itself as fascination. As one of the many listeners who heeds the man—even if I'm more an intermittent partisan than a tour-list following tracking aficionado—I remain drawn in, intrigued. Because if the songs lay out a true lyric map of our era, the artist himself appears to be forever skirting the consequentiality of his inspiration, or bracketing it, or refusing overt image-identification with it. He has simply not accepted—indeed has at every point flouted—the expected mapping of appearance to what we like to think of as reality. He has created an uncertain, often agitated—but at other times stony-cold—presence that shimmers ectoplasmically in front of the music.

I don't want to overstate. Dylan is by no means a playful show-man chameleon, though at points in his career he has tried this on as well—think of the white-face of the Rolling Thunder tour. No, the presence is often a calculated distancing, a way of throwing up a wall between performing a song and claiming its emotion—its verbal passion—for his own. Some of this must be self-protective, having to do with his ever-grueling performance schedule, often as many as two hundred shows a year. For whatever reason, Dylan takes his music on the road far more than his reputation, or his bank account, would presumably require. But this in itself is part of the disjunction, a feature of the mystery. Why does the man perform so much? Is it a penance? Or, as he has sometimes claimed, a way of vocally revising the songs? I don't know. But certainly he keeps himself publicly removed and changeful in a way that makes me think that there might be a mysterious third narrative unfolding between what we hear and what we consume as image.

This brings me back to that unfortunate semiotic phrase and the idea behind it, which is that that whole elaborate ballet of shifting public personae changes its nature the moment we isolate the idea of the actual—that which has always lain implicitly behind the changing faces as enigma, but which now, for whatever reason, seems to be revealing itself. Revealing itself not only in Dylan's decision to appear without masks, *as himself*, for Scorsese's film, but also more or less concurrently on the larger timeline, by writing his memoir, *Chronicles* (2004) in a voice purged of obfuscations and posturings. The prose is marked by its unvarnished casualness, its overt refusal to be straining for effect. Of course, as I said before, both self-presentations, on screen and page, could be instances of the most insidious put-on of all—putting on a self that appears, for once, to not be putting itself on—but I prefer to think not. I'd rather have it that the man has reached a point in his life where he feels free—emboldened—to risk being himself. Why this should be the case—now, in late middle age—is anybody's guess.

It is not, I imagine, an easy or natural shift, not a simple matter of turning off the artifice-switch. Artifice is not assumed quite that readily or directly, not in this case; artifice is more like a personality style, a way of being that develops out of a compelling inner need. Dylan's dropping of facades, in other words, is not the same as an actor's letting go of a part, though I would add that seeing him 'unplugged' in the Scorsese film has some of the feel of seeing a character-identified actor answering questions about his craft.

But with this comparison things get more complicated. For an actor, being interviewed in shirtsleeves will reflect on his work, his roles, his inhabiting of, say, Hannibal Lecter. But Dylan, to my knowledge, has not closed the circle; he has never really gone public about the relentless metamorphoses that have defined his public career. Rather, in showing himself for who he is, he has simply stopped being who he's not, bringing forward the 'natural sign' (another semiotic concept, as I recall), almost as if this face were simply the latest in the ongoing sequence. But no, after this, after the shedding of all masks and with them the idea of pretense, there is no going back; no later return to masked performances.

While I think of this self-exposure as being bold, or risky, my feeling as I watch those sections is also of a strange kind of flattening. The shock is in the *fact* of the difference more than in the presentation itself. That Dylan, talking, answering questions, should have to fumble for phrases like the rest of us. That Dylan, so lyrical and strange in his songs (many of them), should write a simple, straight, matter-of-fact prose: "Topical songs weren't protest songs. The term 'protest singer' didn't exist any more than the term 'singer-songwriter.' You were a performer or you weren't, that was about it—a folksinger or not one."

The contrast not only tells on Dylan, on our fantasies and projections, but it also deepens the split between the idiom of the artist-'inspired' and the artist in day-to-day mode. Dylan coming to us in an ordinary voice underscores like nothing else the 'otherness' of the songwriter. Between the prose and the lyrics is a great gulf.

Studying the face of the 65 year-old man, I'm fixated on the intertwined mysteries of self-making and impersonation. At what moment does a person coin a new name for himself, and when, if ever, does he gain title to it? Seen in the right light, the issue is fascinating. For an emerging performer to change his or her name to something more catchy is a career decision; it makes marketing sense. For a teen-aged boy to invent, claim, and then begin to inhabit a name is something else again. The shift from Robert Zimmerman to Bob Dylan tells us a good deal about his aspirations. On the one hand, it is a move toward the plainspoken/casual ('Bob' not 'Robert' Dylan), on the other toward the 'poetic' (Dylan Thomas).

Dylan uses a wonderful phrase in the film to describe his younger self. He was, he says several times, "a musical expeditionary." This is not a word I recognize as a noun, and I'm tempted to look it up. But I won't, preferring to think of it as Dylan's ad hoc coinage. "Expeditionary." Meaning what? One who goes on musical expeditions? That would make a certain obvious sense, except that the way Dylan uses it, the context, which is all about the young singer's enormous zeal for absorbing influences from all directions—indeed, borrowing and not returning large quantities of records from friends in Minneapolis (among them Tony "Little Sun" Glover of Koerner, Ray & Glover fame)—makes me wonder if there might not be a hint of "expedience" stirred in. What comes through loud and clear is that the Dylan of those early years was a magpie, a borrower, a gypsy, a poacher. Enough years have passed by the time of filming to allow Dave Van Ronk (he has since died) to be bemused, though clearly still nettled, as he recounts how Dylan appropriated his arrangement of "House of the Risin' Sun" for his first album. But stories like Van Ronk's abound. David Hajdu's eye-opening *Positively 4th Street* explores at some length how the artist piggy-backed on the reputation of the then-far-more-famous Joan Baez.

Dylan never stopped, never let up; his artistic ambition was formidable. Formidable, but also very much at odds with the ethos of the folk scene, which was populist and collective right down to its manifestly radical roots. As was, let's note, Dylan's own image in those early years. He was creating himself as the Woody-inspired ramblin' boy, the work-shirted proletarian, never mind that Woody himself was never on the make, and that his populism was genuinely about helping the poor. Dylan sang "Pretty Boy Floyd," but he did so while elbowing his way to the front of the line.

But it's too easy somehow to call him a phony or a poseur, though both labels are gummy enough to stick. To me it makes more sense to study the contradiction as just that. Not, in other words, a case of a false front laid upon a less attractive reality, but of two drives in tense opposition. What's more, I would argue that this face-off of polarized selves—the idealist and the climber—allowed, even encouraged, the public procession of masks and poses. The more he changed his pitch, the less he was invested in its implications. So long as he was in one of his enigmatic guises, Dylan was free of having to account for the contradiction, either to others or to himself. The image could become an arena of freedom.

Of course this is only a supposition, but it does help me understand why in a movie like D.A. Pennebaker's *Don't Look Back* (Scorsese's title makes an interesting echo), the singer comes across as so impossibly antic, such a tightly compacted bundle of warring energies. On the one hand he is wooing his British audiences, on the other he is snarling and writhing, at every moment trying to shake off the expectation that he *be* this or that. Thrown into the dense sociability of the tour—with Baez, Allen Ginsberg, Donovan, Albert Grossman, or the dozens of hangers-on who haunt his room—he can be seen constantly absenting himself, drawing away to sit at the piano, or at his typewriter. His art, at those moments, seems almost less an avenue of creative expression than a shield against the first breaking waves of his fame. That first movie is remarkable for various reasons, not least for the fact that Dylan does not show himself even once without the armor—without sarcasm, silliness, teasing, verbal gamesmanship, nonsensical assertion, or one of his other performing postures.

The same is true of most of the clips we see in Scorsese's film, except for the surprise of the present-day interview clips. What makes these last so fascinating, in part, is Dylan's own detachment from his various younger personae. Where he once launched his sardonic, cynical, brooding front at the world, now he comments back with a kind of wry indulgence, almost disavowing, locating his younger self in fondly distanced anecdote. As the young Dylan left Zimmerman behind in Hibbing, so this recent-vintage Dylan puts miles between himself and that former version of himself. Watching the face closely, we can't help but notice that he is constantly at war with his own impulse to smile.

Another night of watching… I'm no longer following the film from start to finish so much as just checking in on it, collaging it like a favorite CD. It doesn't seem to matter that I dip in this way—I don't know that there is a binding shape to what Scorsese has done. Or if there is, the intensity of my local absorption and my associative 'bleeds' off to this side or that make the idea of a larger documentary unit almost irrelevant. I notice two things. One: that it seems to make no difference to my involvement at what point I enter: I have no interest in the 'narrative' beyond what I already know of the basic career evolution. And two: that my appetite for plunging into any particular scene is, at least so far, inexhaustible. Though I know the footage well, I don't get bored or impatient. I look and look, drinking in whatever is in front of me, zeroing in on different things each time. So it will likely be so long as I regard Dylan as an enigma, a mystery to be solved.

One of these clues is the mouth. The more I watch, the more my eye is drawn to the lips, how they move while Dylan is talking and singing. The mouth is a 'tell'—there is some way in which it doesn't seem comfortable, just isn't right. Tense. I see it as the focused site of Dylan's extreme self-consciousness. When he is talking, especially, the lips seem unnaturally tight, not at ease with the words they are forming. Sometimes he seems at the point of smirking, at other times I see him clamping back on some afterthought or correction.

This tension proposes a rich paradox. For Dylan is one of our bards, one of our truth-telling visionaries, the artist for whom the words are everything. What does it mean that the instrument of his expression is not relaxed—in sync with its expressions—but clenched up? Again, I'm thrown back on the idea of a split, a collision of opposing energies. On one hand, the drive to give voice to a profound, highly-charged vision of the world, and on the other a competing impulse to dissimulate, to tell it slant. This has to do with more than just facial discomfort. It somehow also connects with the gulf, the disjunction, between the level of verbal articulation in the songs, and the often halting, obstructed, generalizing speaking-self. Romantic as it may sound, I often think that the composition of the music and lyrics originates in a different register of the self—not exactly the Muse of former days, but her psychological equivalent. If this is in any degree true, then the performing—and speaking—Dylan must register the split, possibly to the extent of feeling like an impostor in the face of his gift.

I find it interesting, in this light, to watch the clips of the young Dylan singing some of his early protest songs, like "The Lonesome Death of Hattie Carroll," or "Only a Pawn in their Game." Until you really study him more closely he seems passably earnest—an understated idealist who is muting all stage affect in order to convey the seriousness of his message. Of course that's the style—the pose—of the day. Certainly it's what his folkie public, and his influential elders (Pete Seeger, The Weavers) wanted from him. In one sequence, Dylan is singing at Newport, singing "Mr. Tambourine Man"—controversially secular, lyrical, *not* political—and we see a young Pete Seeger squatting on his heels just behind him on the stage, tapping his foot slightly, but as vigilant as a commissar in his facial expressions. Could he be vetting for authenticity? Is he registering the full transgression underway, the turn represented by those "smoke-rings" of the mind?

Dylan tried to dissociate himself from protest over and over, but it was almost as if the supreme folkie committee wouldn't let him go. After all, he had written all the songs—"Blowin' in the Wind," "The Times They Are A-changin'"—how would it look if he stepped away? It's almost as if the man had to go electric just to get their attention, so that he could make it clear to the inside circle, as well as the larger world, that he did not want to be tied to the cause as a spokesman. Not because his artist's heart didn't belong to the oppressed—at the deeper generative level perhaps it did—but because he felt a larger ambition, one that included but also went beyond the sectarian-political. And if we think of it this way, the expression, the sober intensity of those early outings at the mike, can almost be seen as an impersonation by one who knows he is biding his time.

The longer I work at writing, the more I trust and treasure the interventions of serendipity, which is not, of course, some purely divine strike of accident, but rather the happy filling of a need, which only happens when that need has made itself inwardly evident. This does not necessarily mean that it has become *conscious*. In my case, I was writing about the image, what I imagine to be the public and private face of Bob Dylan, but my concept of the masks and the face behind the masks somehow didn't feel rich enough, didn't answer to my sense of mystery. But then—the gods took pity—I went to visit a friend, and this woman, a photographer and writer, asked me how my project was going. I naturally vented my frustrations and doubts, brought up my whole fixation with the face, the image. This, in turn, put us on a track; we started speculating, doing what all Dylan fans do, revisiting ourselves by way of favorite songs and lines, remarking the cruel passage of years, only gradually finding our way back to my topic. There was a moment's pause before my friend looked at me and said: "You haven't mentioned the main thing. The main thing is that he was just so beautiful."

Beautiful. That stopped me for a few seconds—two responses were instantly superimposed. One was: "Dylan—beautiful?" The other, possibly faster and more decisive was "Of course!" I knew exactly what she meant, over and above the first dissenting reflex: "That skinny, scraggly-haired kid, *beautiful?*" But he was, utterly and absolutely, to the point where—so clear once I admitted it—it was the overwhelming unvoiced recognition of my watching. Bob Dylan was

in so many ways arresting, radiant, completely stunning to contemplate. This was the heart of my response to Scorsese's film. This was
what allowed me to return to those familiar moments over and over.
I had told myself it was because I was being a detective, processing
evidence, taking in the subtle dissonance between the performing
affect and the contents. And to be sure, there was some of that. But
really it was beauty I was staring at. For isn't it the nature of beauty
that we want to be in its presence, that we don't—can't—tire of it?
We don't—can't—because it communicates not a message but a sense
of essence.

But I was also curious. My friend had seen the film. "Do you mean
that all of Dylan is beautiful, or—?"

"Oh no—no, I mean that boy, that young boy up on the stage
with Joan Baez, all those scenes—"

"So not the present-day Dylan, the one who looks like an
embezzler?"

She laughed. "Certainly not—at least not in the way I mean."

Here I knew I'd gotten it all wrong. Or, if not wrong, then at least
I was woefully incomplete. Struck by many of the same moments,
I had fooled myself. I had dressed my reaction up as nostalgia. The
powerful feeling I got watching Dylan in front of a mike with Joan
Baez, or singing by himself at the Washington march, or at Newport,
or in England—I had told myself it was nostalgia, pure and simple.

Nostalgia: she gave me another word for it. But nostalgia is there,
too—nostalgia, the root meaning of which is, from the Greek, 'the
longing for home.' Home, for which there is no direction, for which
there is only the desire that grows in proportion to our distance.

I will come back to this idea, but first there is the beauty question.
How is it that this thin and bony-faced singer—that boy whom any
good Jewish mother would want to stuff with blintzes—is beautiful?
To answer is to move straight away off the conventional, for this is

no paradigmatic pretty-boy. If he is beautiful it's because the face, the mobile performing face, even masked as it is, communicates an intensity and clarity that the soul finds irresistible. At least my soul does. Young Dylan singing gives off a pure radiance, not the ghost of electricity, but the real thing. Watching the clips from the early 60s it is obvious as can be that he will become a star. And everyone back then said so, too. Joan Baez can't get enough of recalling what wattage he put out. Is it self-evident—the intensity, the genius, that is also the beauty? How much does it have to do with the fresh power of the songs themselves? Would I feel the same if I didn't have the name 'Bob Dylan,' if he were singing 'C.C. Rider' instead of 'Chimes of Freedom'? But also, as important, does this perception square with my prior conviction that Dylan is never not acting, never not holding up one of his calculated façades?

Face or façade—its strangely glowing familiarity has somehow presided over my life. If not 'presided,' then been steadily present, intimate and puzzling. And I've spent a good deal of time staring and wondering, trying to figure my way to the root of my connection. Thanks to my friend, I now get that, at some level, I've been responding to beauty, a realization that pulls me right back into the mysteries of expression. Whether it is a mask or the essential thing, what I see I see as the face of the man who makes the music, who writes and sings the songs. And this can only pull me back to my very earliest listening, that time of peak vulnerability when I was not only moved by what I heard, but I took up a kind of occupancy there. *The Freewheelin' Bob Dylan*—my first—that Columbia album with its red label, spinning at 33 r.p.m. through the afternoons and nights when I was 16. There is no way to understand this without wondering just how the floating emotional self inscribes itself, its own obscure sense of fatality, into the scenarios conjured by the lyrics. So little was needed. I took the bare-bones longing of a song like 'Girl from the North Country' and I decked them out with everything I knew and imagined about love, loneliness, sacrifice, regret… I don't think I can get much more specific: these events—gaining through endless repetition—happen on the frequency of daydream and desire. They're not fully-fledged thoughts, or even scenes. Less substantial, they are inward waxings and wanings that take place around the shift from a major to a minor chord, somehow soaking the available contents of the self in formation.

I had responded deeply to Dylan back then, long before I knew anything more of the look, the image, than what was there to be contemplated on the album cover. But the transfer took, and the proof is undeniably here in the fixation of a fifty-four year-old man upon the face of a twenty year-old singer. Nostalgia does play into the response, no question. Complex nostalgia—for a back-then, for myself when young, for a raw state of possibility that underlay everything that would come later, and that maps, imprecisely, to all the possibility that Dylan himself embodied. For he was himself in his first germination, the enormity of his fame and influence, as well as the extent of his explosive talent, still hidden from him. The power of retrospect to infuse what was with what will be—the perspective of the gods.

Alongside the personal nostalgia, the ineffable tropism toward the self *before*, is the collective historical pull. The times, how we all were, the world as we knew it then. And here Dylan has an ensemble role, really. He is there with all the others, his face alongside Ginsberg's, Seeger's, Baez's, Van Ronk's, his physical presence there in the ambushed atmospherics of the times, reminding us that the more vivid, more poignant world was still unfolding in black and white. Dylan at the mike with Baez, Dylan at Club 47 in Cambridge, lifting young Baez off her feet and carrying her. The heart-stopping spectacle of all that youth, with all the erosions and undoings of time still in the wings, not even surmised.

But here is Dylan again, the man as he looks now, that radiance completely effaced, remade, the face turned retrospective, sly, self-deprecating. If there is any beauty now it is the beauty of wisdom, the 'heads or tails' possibility finally settled on the counter-top. But I realize that I'm every bit as compelled by this face, if for completely different reasons. The latest Dylan gives off a difficult beauty, but one that fairly vibrates with the ironies of its self-contemplation. It offers a completely different promise. This man is no longer the cipher of possibility, but rather the idea of arrival, possibility having been claimed and lived through, the man on the other side, having come through, having at last dropped the masks that stood guard over the gambles of change. *No Direction Home* is a natural choice for a title—so very Dylan—but I don't know if it is completely accurate. It gets the prodigal's profound restlessness, his outward momentum, yes, but it too readily rules out the return trip—which seems to be the power of those astonishing recent clips.

(2006)

Interiors

My eyes open in the dark.

There's not even the slightest paling along the edges of the window shades. I'm tempted to say it's pitch-black, but it's not. It's just that I haven't begun to see. Soon enough, I'll start to differentiate the least granular variations, one area of the ceiling totally dark, another fronting the bookcases shading dimly gray. At this point there's no more chance of sleep. I'm up.

"Up" means I will see it all, the first milky trace, and with it the dark's powdery substance. If I stare with full concentration, I'll follow the stages, the day slowly pressing against the window, the things in the room detaching one by one from night, taking on contour, like the lampshade incrementally outlined, the wall behind it lightening, and soon enough the edge of the wooden desk, the metallic sheen bringing out the profile of my desk chair.

On it goes, the places where the light first lands shifting slightly from one morning to the next, but after a week or so, it's clear: the Earth follows a path around the sun. I close my eyes to rest for a moment. When I open them again, I am fully in my room.

~

I went through a period of convalescence recently, spending much of the day in bed—this on top of the general sequestration that so many of us have been going through, each in our own way. I felt I was rediscovering the objects around me, resting my gaze on one thing and another for so long it seemed I could trace the nuances of shape and assess weight and feel—all from memory. The things were things I knew, but after the usual brushing glances, I could now fasten on them and rouse them, as if they had been locked in sleep instead of me. Each thing was now present unto itself—the convalescent's ad-hoc phenomenology.

I remember sick days from my childhood, my mother's cool hand on my forehead, the thermometer, then her voice in the other room making the call to my school; and after that, the slightly illicit dreaminess of realizing the morning bus had come and gone. Strange to be in bed with the morning light coming in the windows, left alone, except now and then my mother looming over me to check my forehead, or bringing toast and juice, an aspirin. Never again have I drifted unmoored for that long, the world so far away, the window-light changing, feeling I'm on some great ship moving through space. I go lightly into sleep and emerge effortlessly. At some point I come face-to-face with the knowing: this is me.

In the hours I've been lying here, silence has carved away everything else.

~

This period of confinement seemed like a good time to go through the family photos I've inherited—all those carefully curated albums, the boxes, and then the big brown envelopes packed with miscellaneous images from every era, some going back past color and black-and white and coming to rest in sepia, in the time when the taking of a photograph was an occasion. The concept of zeitgeist, if not the word itself, was in my thoughts as I shuffled and sorted. It was hard

for me not to think that way. The sepia photos from Latvia in the early
1900s, black and-whites from my parents' war years in Germany, and
then—how fitting—the first bursts of color coinciding with their
arrival in America.

The differences from decade to decade make vivid the shifts in
our ways of living in the world. I consider the personal, but really I
mean the feeling of the times as experienced collectively, over and
above any person's particular version of things—the so-called "spirit
of the times."

We usually catch this spirit in retrospect. It is fused with certain
songs, fashions, and jingles. Encountering them later we realize we've
moved along—that everything has changed. Characterizing labels have
been created and our memories begin to conform, and so we ride
forward through the eras, each with its touchstones and atmospheres.

A zeitgeist is a vortex, pulling events and these tones into a
remembered coherence. Predictably, these distinct-seeming periods
are often marked by larger calamities: the market crash, World War II,
Vietnam, 9/11—shocking events that dictated how we paid attention.

Our particular period—where we are right now—feels too vast
and unresolved to be called a phase. It is changing everyone, creating
a new zeitgeist, and ensuring that the fantasy of a return to former
ways is just that. When it recedes from us, the scars will be visible.

When people can take up their lives fully again, where will we
be? I can't yet imagine. So many things will become clear only when
the danger is past, when we can assess the ways we've been branded.
Will we share a new collective outlook? Will we Americans keep any
of the traces of our celebrated innocence? If that innocence—that
credulity—disappears, how will the old engines proceed? How will
advertisers push their products, their travel packages—all the things
that ride on the bright smile and the implication that the future will be
better than the past? These are the sorts of things I wondered about
in my room, looking out the window.

~

The idea of a room signifies variously. I think right away of Pascal and his declaration: "All of humanity's problems stem from man's inability to sit quietly in a room alone." This is not so true in our time of living indoors—the problems only seem to be growing—but we know what he means. Pascal saw a room as an enclosure, a place of solitude away from the chaotic circus surrounding. I note the emphasis on *alone*. He is talking about the cultivation of inwardness. A room, in this sense, is a version of Voltaire's garden. It represents personal fulfillment, a restoration of proportion, a kind of tending. Attending.

And Virginia Woolf? The room in her famous title represented independence for women, a haven for creativity, a counterpart to the club rooms catering exclusively to men. It was a seat of power, a profession of self, a place where introspection could flourish, away from the old expectations of what a woman ought to be doing with her time. Again, I hear the assertion of solitude. Where Pascal spoke of being "alone" in a room, Woolf makes clear that the room is "one's own." She proposes a cultivated individuality.

Montaigne in his book-lined tower—room as a contemplative retreat—looked back on his life and mused on whatever topics came to mind. And from that perch, aimed to do so philosophically, *sub specie aeternitatis*, the altitude of the tower room encouraging vantage and perspective, the literal sight-line taken inward.

It's impossible not to invoke Proust here too, the most famous literary room-occupant ever. The man spent much of his adult life self-sequestered in a special cork-lined space. For him, the room was the way to silence the world, push it distant enough that his inwardness could prosper, allowing the buried past to be raised from the deeps by the taste of a dampened tea-cake.

~

Memory—sinuous and resinous, the molten sap that becomes amber. The cork room allowed Proust the interiority that could hold it all. He needed the solitude, the sequestration. Where are such conditions to be found now, outside the monastic orders? How might they be self-imposed, and to what end? I think first of those who would create art. Musicians, painters, writers. Artists take what the work demands—however much will allow focus as well as freedom of thought. As Yeats wrote in "Long-Legged Fly," picturing Michelangelo on his scaffold, painting: "Like a long-legged fly upon the stream / His mind moves upon silence." In Yeats' conception, silence is a kind of plenum, an undivided element that allows one to bring the attention to a fine point. Not the absence of sound so much as the absence of distraction.

That inwardness is harder to reach in our day. I don't need to trot out all the cliché observations about screen life, wormholes, action at a tap. But looking out the window, I did wonder about this. Has our long spell of social isolation driven us deeper into our various online recourses, or has it, for some, triggered the contrary impulse, goading us to explore the seductions of introversion?

~

In my room-bound days, as afternoon came on, I would stop, setting aside whatever I'd been doing, and open myself once again to looking. The window beside the bed caught the best afternoon light, and the bare wall opposite was open to shadows. The shadows arrived without fail when there was sun—slithery amoebic shapes that moved along slowly, almost like clouds across a summer sky, one after another. Filmy, glowing and fading, every so often they would gather into formations of startling beauty. I would reach for my iPhone and, holding still like a hunter, wait for the right moment. I realized one day that a room was, at least etymologically, a camera—camera *meant* room, it was the Latin for an enclosure with an arched ceiling. I was in a camera with a camera, but for all that I could never capture what I wanted. I would bring the phone close to my face and stare at the images on the small screen—sharpen, adjust, tinker with the vibrancy. But what had slid across the wall and made such a display was not to be held or translated into a fixed shape. Shadows in the room, like thoughts in the daydreamer's mind . . .

(2022)

Acknowledgments

My gratitude to Bill Pierce, who worked his skills with the greatest care, Shuchi Saraswat, Brad Morrow, Tom Frick, Askold Melnyczuk, Rob McQuilkin, Christopher Benfey, and Jennifer Alise Drew. Special thanks to Ezra Fox for his editorial and design savvy, and to Catherine Parnell and the team at *Arrowsmith* for their work and dedication.

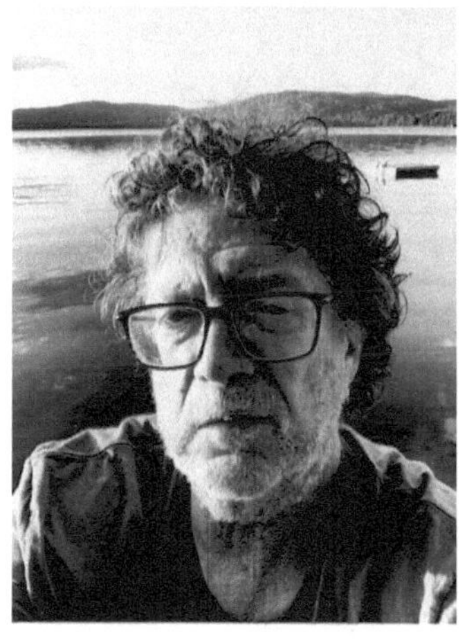

Sven Birkerts is the author of eleven books of essay and memoir, including *The Gutenberg Elegies* and *Changing the Subject: Art and Attention in the Internet Age*. He is the former Director of the Bennington Writing Seminars and the co-editor of the journal *AGNI*. He lives in Amherst with his wife Lynn.

Books by

ARROWSMITH
PRESS

Girls by Oksana Zabuzhko

Bula Matari/Smasher of Rocks by Tom Sleigh

This Carrying Life by Maureen McLane

Cries of Animals Dying by Lawrence Ferlinghetti

Animals in Wartime by Matiop Wal

Divided Mind by George Scialabba

The Jinn by Amira El-Zein

Bergstein
edited by Askold Melnyczuk

Arrow Breaking Apart by Jason Shinder

Beyond Alchemy by Daniel Berrigan

Conscience, Consequence: Reflections on Father Daniel Berrigan
edited by Askold Melnyczuk

Ric's Progress by Donald Hall

Return To The Sea by Etnairis Rivera

The Kingdom of His Will by Catherine Parnell

Eight Notes from the Blue Angel by Marjana Savka

Fifty-Two by Melissa Green

Music In—And On—The Air by Lloyd Schwartz

Magpiety by Melissa Green

Reality Hunger by William Pierce

Soundings: On The Poetry of Melissa Green
edited by Sumita Chakraborty

The Corny Toys by Thomas Sayers Ellis

Black Ops by Martin Edmunds

Museum of Silence by Romeo Oriogun

City of Water by Mitch Manning

Passeggiate by Judith Baumel

Persephone Blues by Oksana Lutsyshyna

The Uncollected Delmore Schwartz
edited by Ben Mazer

The Light Outside by George Kovach

The Blood of San Gennaro by Scott Harney
edited by Megan Marshall

No Sign by Peter Balakian

cont...

Firebird by Kythe Heller

The Selected Poems of Oksana Zabuzhko
edited by Askold Melnyczuk

The Age of Waiting by Douglas J. Penick

Manimal Woe by Fanny Howe

Crank Shaped Notes by Thomas Sayers Ellis

The Land of Mild Light by Rafael Cadenas
edited by Nidia Hernández

The Silence of Your Name: The Afterlife of a Suicide by Alexandra Marshall

Flame in a Stable by Martin Edmunds

Mrs. Schmetterling by Robin Davidson

This Costly Season by John Okrent

Thorny by Judith Baumel

The Invisible Borders of Time: Five Female Latin American Poets
edited by Nidia Hernández

Some of You Will Know by David Rivard

The Forbidden Door: The Selected Poetry of Lasse Söderberg
tr. by Lars Gustaf Andersson & Carolyn Forché

Unrevolutionary Times by Houman Harouni

Between Fury & Peace: The Many Arts of Derek Walcott
edited by Askold Melnyczuk

The Burning World by Sherod Santos

Today is a Different War: Poetry of Lyudmyla Khersonska
tr. by Olga Livshin, Andrew Janco, Maya Chhabra, & Lev Fridman

Salvage by Richard Kearney

In the Hour of War: Poetry From Ukraine
edited by Carolyn Forché and Ilya Kaminsky

A Crash Course in Molotov Cocktails: Poetry of Halyna Kruk
tr. by Amelia Glaser and Yuliya Ilchuk

Don't Close Your Eyes by Hanna Melnyczuk

Tiny Extravaganzas by Diane Mehta

Departures from Rilke by Steven Cramer

On the Road to Lviv by Christopher Merrill
tr. into Ukrainian by Nina Murray

Nothing Bad Has Ever Happened
A Bouquet to Victoria Amelina

The Farewell Light by Nidia Hernández

Downfall of the Straight Line by Charles O. Hartman

The God of Freedom by Yulia Musakovska
tr. Olena Jennings and the author

Away Away by Mark Pawlak

Arrowsmith is named after the late William Arrowsmith, a renowned classics scholar, literary and film critic. General editor of thirty-three volumes of *The Greek Tragedy in New Translations*, he was also a brilliant translator of Eugenio Montale, Cesare Pavese, and others. Arrowsmith, who taught for years in Boston University's University Professors Program, championed not only the classics and the finest in contemporary literature, he was also passionate about the importance of recognizing the translator's role in bringing the original work to life in a new language.

Like the arrowsmith who turns his arrows straight and true,
a wise person makes his character straight and true.

— Buddha

www.ingramcontent.com/pod-product-compliance
Lightning Source LLC
Chambersburg PA
CBHW031045160726
47991CB00005B/2034